Praise for Karen Taylor Bass

Expert public relations maven Karen Taylor Bass IS the Mother of Reinvention. Her own life is a testament to setting goals, achieving them, having a great career, finding love, getting married, becoming a mother of two and managing the juggle with style, substance and success.

— *Dyana Williams is a seasoned broadcaster, celebrity strategist and mother to three amazing people!*

Karen Taylor Bass has the unique art of combining passion with expertise! From a premier PR expert to the reinvention of a multimedia maven she's never been afraid to step outside her comfort zone. Now she'll share her unique vision for success in Reinvention Mom/PR Expert.

— *Sheila Eldrige, CEO of MilesAhead Entertainment*

Karen has an uncanny ability to take something as heavy as post childbirth confidence, and turn it into something fun, light-hearted, and even empowering!

— *Akilah S. Richards, Lifestyle Coach, TheLifeDesignAgency.com.*

Karen Taylor Bass is master at "reinvention" and this book will show you how you too can rediscover yourself after a major life shift. I have seen Karen work her magic for celebrities as a publicist, now I'm amazed at how she hit the reset button—and changed her brand entirely. Get inspired and fired up!

— *Pam Perry, PR Coach & Social Media Strategist, www.pamperrypr.com*

ISBN# 0-9759106-3-9

Price: $16.95 (USA)
$19.95 (Canada)

The Brand New Mommy: From Babies To Branding To Bliss
(Learn how to renew your life)

By Karen Taylor Bass

TaylorMade Books
Valley Stream, NY 11582-0099
www.thebrandnewmommy.com
www.karentaylorbass.com
www.taylormademediapr.com

Copyright © 2012 by Karen Taylor Bass. All rights reserved

Library of Congress Cataloging-in-Publication Data

No part of this book may be reproduced in any form or by any electronic or mechanical means including information storage and retrieval systems, without permission in writing from the author.

For more information contact: *info@thebrandnewmommy.com*

Design: Straight Design, www.str8tdesign.com
Cover illustration: Yogy Ikhwanto/iStockphoto
Copy Editor: Astrid Roy Pinto
Social Media PR: Pam Perry, Ministry Marketing Solutions, Inc.

Printing: CreateSpace.com
First printing: October 2012

ISBN: 0-9759106-3-9

THE 'BRAND' NEW MOMMY:
FROM BABIES TO BRANDING TO BLISS
(learn how to renew your life)

By Karen Taylor Bass

TaylorMade Books

TABLE OF CONTENTS

Acknowledgments	xi
Thank You's	xii
Praise for Karen Taylor Bass	xiii
Foreword by Jill Scott	xiv
Introduction	xv

Act I : Babies
The real deal dirt on motherhood—the good, bad, sad and blessings

Old Habits	1
Who is a brand new mommy?	2
Branding on Bed Rest	3
Jilly from Philly talks Baby, Balance, and Branding	5
Mocha Moms are More than just Mothers	7
Five Tips to a Stress-free Holiday: Blended Family Style!	9
Check to see if you need a time-out?	10
Why Friends Change with Motherhood?	11
Understand and Recognize Moms's Silent Killer	12
Mommy Back to School Tips	14
Paula Patton Talks Lip Gloss	15
Motherhood the Second Time Around at 40	16

Act II : Branding
Understanding the power of your emotions and actions

3 Power Ways to Kickoff your Style with Kimora Lee Simmons	19
Five Ways to Stay Mentally Charged!	20
7 Tips to Marketing Your Authentic Self	21
Nine Steps for Working Smoothly With Friends and Family	23
Nine Tips to Becoming the Next Terry McMillian	25
Ten Tips for Writing a Winning E-Book	27
A Polished Image improves Brand Confidence	29
Blueprint for Success	31
Brand Age: Lessons to Learn from Demi Moore	33
Brush Off Your Old Way of Thinking	34
Is this 'Brand' new mommy stuck?	36
Lessons Learned from 'Brand' J-Hudson	37

Jumpstarting Your Personal Brand After Mommy-hood	38
Mentorship is as Important as Oxygen	40
Is Your Brand, Bold, Beautiful & Determined?	42
Positioning Yourself for an Opportunity	44
Pro Bono Mommy: Stop Giving Away your Expertise	46
Score A-List Public Relations on a Shoestring Budget, Part I	47
Score A-List Public Relations on a Shoestring Budget, Part II	49
Re-Invention After The Storm	51
Social Media: The New Currency	53
Speed Networking: Brand and Promote in 2 Minutes	55
Yolanda Adams Gets Comfortable in Her Skin	57
Brand Mom: Tips To Maximize 2.5 Hours	59
Date Yourself	60
Don't Give Away Your M&Ms (Mind & Muscle)	61
What is 'Kitty' Power, Do Moms Have It?	62
JLo's Divorce 'Branding Tips'	64

Act III : Bliss
Reset the mind, body, soul and spirit

Living for You: Maximize this Weekend!	67
Divinely Imperfectly Imbalance is the New Black!	68
Brand New Mommy Bliss Tip: Timing is Everything...Can't Rush Process	69
Celebrate Valentine's Day with Mommy Self-Love!	70
Gratitude: Give Some and Get Some	71
Moms: Need Personal Time Too	72
Breathing is a Gift	73
Countdown to 8:30	74
Celebrate Your Bliss!	75
I Am Thankful	76
Why We Love Our Girlfriends	77
Dear 'Brand' New Mommy	78
About the Author	81
Resources for The 'Brand' New Mommy	82
Order Information	83

Acknowledgments

Five years ago, I was sitting in my living room breastfeeding my daughter, Sofia, when God planted the seed of the 'brand' new mommy.

Thank you to everyone in my life who has been a positive and not so positive influence. You inspire me to be REAL.

Experiencing childbirth at 40 has been the greatest gift and the most challenging. I lost self and had to press reset to create a better 'brand' and Karen.

I dedicate this book and all that I am and will be to my higher power – you carried me when everyone stopped believing—thank you.

My life started (again) when I met Sofia, my inspiration.

The greatest bonus a mom can have, Sebastian, thanks for teaching me patience; a kind and gentle spirit on the low-low is my supportive hubby, Andrew, and he gets a huge shout out.

Lastly, I celebrate the memory of my beloved grandmother, Lurlene Garrick, I miss you more every day.

Thank you and thank you...

I simply want to thank everyone.

My gratitude to the following for allowing me to be me even after the swag was gone.

Love: Andrew, Sebastian and Sofia

Family: Mom, Uncle Kevin, Aunt May, Aunt June, Astrid, Gilda, Aunt Shirley, Christopher, Nyla, momma B, John, Auntie Jeannette, Auntie Winsome, Sharron, Lorne, Yvette and Colin Gayle, Rob, LaTanya, Sabrina, Aisha, Syreeta.

Soul sister: Jill Scott thank you for being my girl and for Amsterdam. LOL

Right Hand Love: Wendy Robinson thank you for always keeping me on path and supporting every vision thus far. Big love.

Little Sister: Darisha Miller you have been an angel and thanks for the media bookings!

Mentor: Coach Beverly Kearney, Dyana Williams and Sheila Eldrige.

Friends: Elayne, Jalila, Pam, Akilah, Agnes, Dr. Renee, Tresa, Karen G., Angie, Janet, Vikki, Danielle T., Lacey!, Tarani, Jalila, Channelle, Lynnette and Earl Cox, Cheryl-Ann Wadlington, Deborah Skinner, Princess Jenkins, Khadija, Rita and Marsha

Media: Christopher Nelson, Patty Jackson, Bobbi Booker, Mina Sabet, *Black Enterprise*, Nate Berkus, *Philadelphia Tribune*, NBC10!, *Essence*, CNN, Jenice Armstrong, *Ebony, The Network Journal*, NBC, FOX, *Amsterdam News, Newsday, NY Daily News*, CBS, BET, WVON.

Organizations: The Brand New Mommy family, Mocha Moms (National), NABJ, BPRS, HBA-NY, University of Texas (Austin), CDA of Hempstead.

Spa Retreat sisters thank you for always trusting and believing in the vision.

Special love to Mocha Moms Queens/Long Island chapter, thank you for saving me when I needed it most.

Dina, my yoga teacher, whom I may not see every week however the chant and intentions are daily.

Foreword

Jill Scott, Grammy Winner, Actress & Mom

This book actually shares the complexity of motherhood ... honestly.

When I was pregnant, I heard only beautiful stories about being a mother; the tender moments, little sweet fingers, softness. I so wanted a child and this little person inside me, was my very own miracle. I was excited, happily fat and full of dreams. I imagined nursing my baby while wind chimes clinked outside. I would glow and feel beautiful. My mother would help me. My grandmother would school me, friends would be on deck to support me and my child's father/my husband would bring me tea and love us both. This would not be my reality.

In actuality, my mother was across the country caring for my sweet grandma Blue. My friends were busy with full, demanding lives and my son's father well...we could hardly bare breathing in the same room. After 36 hours of labor and a vaginal birth, I was sore, exhausted, hormonally unbalanced, emotionally taxed and deeply afraid to be alone. I never felt more alone in my life.

My son Jett and I got home from the hospital when I realized I'd forgotten the prescribed pain meds. I was in terrible pain, bleeding profusely, cranky as hell, still so tired and that angel of mine was SCA-REAM-ING!!! The shrieks were like lightning to my traumatized body. The baby was hungry? (again?). I tried to breast-feed. A lactation consultant came. I tried. Every 15 minutes he screamed. I was going crazy; my poor little person. I had no choice but to supplement. I felt like shit. Nothing was like I thought. Absolutely nothing. My mom was far. My grandmother (and best friend) was dying and the friendship with my son's dad had disintegrated. I wasn't prepared for the sad me. I've always been moderately positive. I always counted the good things gone and prayed for the good things to come. Who was this insanely emotional replica? What had motherhood done to me? I tried to rationalize.

> My grand mother was 91 yrs. old. We know we love each other but...
> I'd been married before. I knew relationships crumble but....
> I have my very own child when doctors told me I never would. I should be happy but...
> I'm not.

I looked at my poor little baby and thought, "I'm already failing you". My ego and my spirit were puddles under the floor. I just wanted to be a great mother, but I wasn't doing too well. I wasn't feeling too good either AND I was wallowing in it. It felt like I was dying. I know it sounds extreme, but that is truly how I felt. I had to choose my child.

I got up, put that baby in the little lamb singing chair thingy (thanx Niecy N) and asked myself what was really really wrong. Ok so he didn't breast feed like I thought, but he's alive aint he? And maybe his father and I didn't make it to forever, but we made a beautiful, healthy boy and he's alive aint he? Shoooot Maybe my friends couldn't drop their lives.

Who the hell was I to ask them to anyway? I was being a punk. I took a long look in the mirror at the new mother I saw and quietly screamed, "Stop bitching and focus". While my baby slept, I cried one more "good" cry. I felt better. I needed rest. I asked friends who love us (Kim M., Jennifer A., Alexis B., Syreeta S., Aisha W.) to come anytime they could for an hour so I could sleep. They did. I felt better. I hired a loving, mature, woman with 3 adult children, a southern background and the skin the color of rich fertile soil to be OUR nanny.

She gave me breaks and a chance to heal. The crying nights became easier. My patience blossomed. I discovered my Jett was lactose intolerant. OH :-(I changed his formula. We felt better. I befriended a trainer (Scott P). I kick boxed thru massive depression and aggression. My ex-fiancé and I communicated (kinda). I went back into the studio. It was cathartic. I could see myself finding a rhythm. I was nurturing to my child, patient with us both. Life got better.

> **I've learned that:**
> *Motherhood is the most demanding job created.*
> *Motherhood is not a dream or a fable etched in the mind.*
> *Nothing is simple when you love someone this much. Nothing is neat when you're this needed*
> *Life doesn't stop because you've given birth.*
> *A new life begins because you have*

My son never got to meet Blue. I sing her song to him. He loves it. My mom (Nay Nay) visits often. They're funny. Jett is 3 now. He's starting school in a few days. He's very creative; so very sweet. He dresses himself and vacuums the sofa. He sings and colors me circles. I like him. I discipline and cuddle him. I praise him and expand his world. I love him. I may do some things differently or backwards. I may even get a little sad but I'm his only Mommy and we're both still alive.

Introduction

At 37, I got married and had an instant family (simply add water and stir).

I decided to leave my hi-profile PR job to enjoy and get to know my new family. My bonus son, Sebastian, had tragically lost his mommy on September 11th. I was determined to love Sebastian and give him the mommy love he needed post September 11.

At 40, God blessed me with a baby and an unpredictable pregnancy; I was diagnosed with placenta previa eight months into my pregnancy, which caused me to be hospitalized and on bed rest for 6 weeks.

I remained prayerful throughout my blessing that all would be well.

I delivered baby Sofia via C-section, experienced internal clotting, which led to 2 blood transfusions and by the miracle of God, I was introduced to my baby nine hours after giving birth.

The journey allowed me to breastfeed for one year, gain 40 pounds and experience mild postpartum. My self-esteem and "brand" plummeted to an all time low.

With the support and coaxing of my husband, I joined a support group and slowly started the healing process, and today I am stronger than ever.

With the economy on the decline, the lack of strategic opportunities for "experienced" public relations professionals I was forced to re-evaluate my next steps.

At the tender age of 43, I experienced an "Aha" moment, after talking to many moms in the same predicament as myself ... moms looking to recapture self, renew and redefine their purpose/brand.

The Brand New Mommy: From Babies To Branding To Bliss is a collection of stories I've written over the past five years, which inspired me daily to reach my ultimate bliss.

I've learned that we (moms) need each other and a reality check often. *The Brand New Mommy: From Babies To Branding To Bliss* was conceived and now delivered to you with love.

Embrace your reinvention, 'brand' new mommy and use this book to create a renewal campaign for you!

The word of the LORD came to me, saying, "Before I formed you in the womb I knew you, before you were born I set you apart; I appointed you as a prophet to the nations."
— *Jeremiah 1:4-5*

"When you stand and share your story in an empowering way, your story will heal you and your story will heal somebody else."
— *Iyanla Vanzant*

Taken from my diary as is with no order…simply healing one moment at a time.

ACT I : BABIES

Having a baby is like winning the lotto—you never know what to expect. Each experience is unique so enjoy yours.

ACT I : BABIES

Old Habits!

As long as I could remember, I was always multi-tasking.
I had so many jobs that the mere thought makes my head spin—from lemonade stand, selling cupcakes and beaded handbags from Thailand to a professional career, this sister was always working and doing too much at an early age.

It should be no surprise that the same working too hard caused me to be diagnosed with Placenta Previa 7 months into my pregnancy and bed rest for 6 weeks.

You would think with all that hustling I would be a millionaire by now. No such luck yet. The common thread is that I was never smart enough to seize the moment, capitalize the present and take a deep breath. Always doing too much but not paying attention.

When I turned 39, I became pregnant unexpectedly, a pure gift. That gift was not enough for me to heed and take my time to enjoy the moment; I had to work and work and save. I continued multi-tasking, running my business, traveling and simultaneously being an uber wife, bonus mom and friend. Life is funny, you can always tell when you are going to crash, the signs are there—I chose to ignore them.

Thankfully, I survived the trauma of hemorrhaging post delivery, clotting, blood transfusions and post partum. My daughter is now 5, healthy, smart, kind and confident.

I am no longer multi-tasking—living in the moment and loving my babies.

Who is a Brand New Mommy™?

It's always important to remember what motivated the fire and measure how ya doing?

Who Is The 'Brand' New Mommy™?

She is every hue of the rainbow and represents the quintessential woman, age ranging from 30-50, and learning each day to find balance as she 're-defines' mommy-hood on her terms and 're-news' her career goals (or launch a new passion).

The 'Brand' New Mommy™ is complex, smart, beautiful, and multi-talented, and, appreciates the simplicity of life (and a splice of the fabulous vida).

The 'Brand' New Mommy™ was once on top of her game pre-babies – now the industry has changed, she has taken time off to raise her children, and learn social media—the new "it" girl. TBNM is coming back stronger, smarter and sensible.

TBNM has to learn the new rules while creating new ones to make her life easier, sustainable and profitable.

The 'Brand' New Mommy™ enjoys making love to her husband/significant other; doting on her children, company, spending time with family, and mentoring the next generation of leaders. TBNM is tre' passionate about finding needed "me" time and relaxing with a glass of vino (Shiraz & Pinot Grigio) and champagne is her spirit of choice.

The 'Brand' New Mommy™ has added some extra cushion to her body courtesy of post-delivery, through it all her girlfriends are her support system. She realizes her health is not a luxury and must work at being fit for life preservation.

The Brand New Mommy™ believes in a higher power and strives to be debt free.

The 'Brand' New Mommy™ will not allow the establishment and others to define her.

She is rewriting the rules, rebuilding her confidence and realizing that in order to do this–she must "re-new" and "re-define" her self as the "brand" new mommy.

If you identify with any or all of the descriptions, guess what? You have landed at thebrandnewmommy.com.

Welcome mommas!

Branding on Bed Rest

Nearly 1 million women in the United States are put on bed rest each year due to pregnancy complications, which can result in preterm birth.

One out of four pregnant women will have a challenging pregnancy; and three out of four Black women will be diagnosed as "high risk" resulting in bed rest.

How do you stay sane, sharp, and empower yourself and your unborn child without getting a little frustrated? You Reinvent.

I resigned from my high profile PR job and decided to treat the diagnosis of bed rest as a time to reinvent a 'brand new' career and live the purposeful life I craved and deserved.

My mission was to reinvent and (finally) pursue my passion as a mommy ambassador, author, and speaker while on bed rest to create a positive experience for her unborn child with bold, courageous 'can-do' thoughts.

I created The Brand New Mommy™ (*www.thebrandnewmommy.com*), a digital destination for savvy women seeking to renew and redefine their personal brand post childbirth.

BRANDING TIPS WHILE ON BED REST:
- **Create A Vision.** Start with a vision board (get a large mounting board, cut out all the photos/magazines and begin to create the life you crave). Bass created a board with images of a safe delivery, healthy baby, living her passion as a speaker, host, financial wealth, loving relationships, affirming words (sky's the limit, optimal wellness) and looked at the vision board each day as she massaged tummy.
- **Girls Day In.** Plan a weekly pajama party in bed with your best girls and have them bring the food, fashion and latest gossip.
- **Go Diva!** Schedule a standing appointment with your nail technician to do a home visit for Mani/Pedi.

- **Write your book.** You have all these ideas now put them to paper and channel that inner novelist.
- **Organize Business Cards.** This is the best time to review all the cards you have collected pre-bedrest and contact all the 'potentials' for business.
- **Tweet to stay sane.** Create your brand and share thoughts with the universe on everything from the latest products to baby names as you create your 'expert' life.

Get rest. A brand-new you and life is right around the corner – get the sleep now.

Jilly From Philly Talks Baby, Balance, and Branding

As you move and groove in life and embark on motherhood in your 30s, the balancing act of family, career and maintaining your personal brand can become a daunting task.

How does one renew and re-define oneself post mommyhood—at age 37—and still maintain top status in the entertainment industry? By being authentic and forgiving for not being perfect.

Jill Scott, our favorite homegirl, multiplatinum, Grammy award-winning singer, poet, author, actress—and now mommy—shares how she balances and enjoys life's golden moments. "Being a mom is better than I thought because of the way I love it and experience how much my son loves me. I wouldn't trade it, however, its work and exhausting."

Scott stresses the importance of having a good support system when raising children. "All women must implement what I call their Operation Village. This is where you assemble your team of family, friends, neighbors and girlfriends to give you a hand and minute to heal. Without my village I would not have made it," she says.

Balance is one of those words that all woman grapple with, and allowing yourself to be human is key to understanding the gift of motherhood. "Women feel like they are supposed to hold it down–that's true to an extent; holding it down does not mean doing it all yourself. Look for people who love and trust you and love your child. You will need time for a walk, replenish your being, and adjust to all the nuances of the mommy-hood. Next to maintaining good health it is essential and mandatory to establish your village for support, " Scott says.

Mommyhood can present older first time moms with a reality check when schedules are no longer theirs and we can easily lose ourselves post delivery. Jill emphatically shares, "I've always done what I wanted to do–If I want to walk, I walk; after 37 years of doing Jill, having a baby threw me—responsibility, sleep deprivation, and exhaustion was r-e-a-l. If you can afford to hire help such as a babysitter and nanny—give yourself that gift—your baby will thank you." BNM, make a promise starting today asking for patience, love, trust and clarity as you design motherhood on your terms.

HERE ARE JILL SCOTT'S 'BRAND' NEW MOMMY TIPS:
- **Know thyself.** I am a sleeper and if I can squeeze in 10 hours I am happy. Take charge and put your baby on a regiment so you can breathe.
- **Work out.** You will feel better and get your body back.
- **Make love.** The physical connection reminds you that you are still a woman and a sexual being and that is equally important as being someone's mommy.
- **Take time for self.** Get out the house and enjoy life— your baby will appreciate a calmer mommy.
- **Give self a lift.** Change hair, change makeup and style to usher in the mommy-hood season.
- **Forgive self.** We are not perfect, and because you want to enjoy life does not mean you are not a good mom – you are a WO-man and must be cherished.

Mocha Moms Are More Than Just Mothers

"Live every day of your life with passion," recommends Mocha Moms (former) President Dee Dee Jackson

Mocha moms of the world unite; we are a movement transforming the home, marketplace and most importantly—self. A mocha mom is a woman of color who has chosen to make parenting and family a priority. She may alter her career, work schedule, or eliminate working outside the home all together to focus on providing the best care for her children—mother care.

And while there are many lower-case mocha moms, there is also the upper-case Mocha Moms Inc., an organization for women learning to re-define their power as it relates to family, community, and self through sisterhood upon leaving their successful careers in corporate America.

Recently, I attended the Mocha Moms Inc., regional conference in Hartford, Connecticut. The energy of the congregation (nearly 100 attendees) was infectious, energetic, loving and practical.

Former president Dee Dee Jackson spoke openly with the moms about making self a priority, recognizing our power as influencers, getting healthy, becoming financially savvy, being a leader in the community, and encouraging one's respective partner daily. "Mochas recognize the sacrifice your husband/mate has made for you to live the life you lead," said Jackson, who was a director for a national HMO before retiring to be home for her children and husband over 10 years ago.

Mocha Moms are all of us—mothers yearning for a better tomorrow for the next generation. Mochas are a force bringing about change and re-defining a "brand" new lifestyle.

Jackson also mentioned that the first step in winning self back is creating a healthy plan for everything you do and want to accomplish. It's okay to start small, however, stay consistent and applaud self for each accomplishment. Mocha Moms are sisters understanding the unexplainable called motherhood.

DEE DEE JACKSON'S NINE GEMS TO EMPOWER ALL MOCHAS TO LIVE A FULFILLED LIFE:
- To thine own self be true.
- Foster loving relationships.
- Seek peace of mind.
- Live a healthy lifestyle.
- Prepare for financial freedom, live debt free, and leave a financial legacy for generations to come.
- Have worthy goals you are working toward and write them down.
- Treat everyone with respect and be of service where you can.
- Live every day of your life with passion and make your desires and dream a reality.
- Live YOUR best life without regret—on purpose!

5 Tips to a Stress-Free Holiday: Blended Family Style!

Let's face it - the traditional American family is no longer.
Just like peanut butter and jelly–America is a blended/stepfamily sandwich. The blended family has become the norm and sometimes when there is much un-channeled energy in a family it can lead to a dramatic holiday.

Stepfamilies, also known as blended families, are more of a norm now than ever, with 65% of remarriages including children from previous relationships. When families "blend" to create stepfamilies, though, things rarely progress smoothly.

Having open communication, positive attitudes, mutual respect, and plenty of love and patience all have an important place in creating a healthy blended family.

One of three Americans is now a stepparent, a stepchild, a stepsibling, or some other member of a blended family. Since 2010 blended families have been the predominant family form in the U.S.

Karen Taylor Bass is a 'bonus' mom with a blended family who has perfected the stress-free holiday celebration.

TAYLOR BASS' TIPS TO A STRESS-FREE THANKSGIVING/CHRISTMAS:
- **Have the 'talk'.** Decide who will host the dinner, carve the turkey and send out invitations.
- **Make a budget.** Nothing spoils an occasion like money drama, set a budget and stick to it.
- **Invite easy-going friends and family,** just in case drama starts, your friends/family can jump in with some laughter.
- **Create a fun activity.** Break out the Pictionary, charade and scrabble to ease the evening with good old fashion competition.
- **Be thankful.** Have your guests share what their thankful for.

Source: www.winningstepfamilies.com/BlendedFamilyStatistics.html

Check to see if you need a time-out?

It's about to be on and poppin' with the crazy holiday festivities, parties, family visits, shopping and not to mention your already packed schedule for the children –how will you find time for you?

Maybe you need a timeout?

You can't concentrate on one task, you're multi-tasking in your sleep, and body aches, feeling a bit run-down, you would pay big bucks for a nap and solace—it's time for a TIMEOUT!

I came off of a well-deserved timeout after the Nate Berkus show pre-post taping for the 'basement reveal.' Coupled with my teaching and traveling schedule, the body took over. A cold was sent my way, which knocked me on my rear and made me take a mandatory timeout. I was freakin' tired.

It's sad when it comes to that, so in the spirit of 'brand' new mommy–I'm taking the afternoon off today (got a babysitter) to bask in a mani/pedi and meet up with hubby later for date night with the Food Network all-stars.

This holiday season is only for a short duration and I vow to do the following for the next twenty plus days. Will you join me?

- **Take a mental timeout.** Shut my noggin down for 5 minutes each morning
- **Walk.** Nothing feels better than an exhilarating power walk.
- **Sip this.** Schedule a little java or Chai with my fave girlfriends.
- **Spa –la-la-la.** Make a date to pamper and spank myself silly with the promo

Why Friends Change with Motherhood?

As I get older I sincerely believe the old adage that everything and everyone has a season and nothing underscores that more than motherhood and friendship.

Friendships change simply because your needs have changed–it's not your fault, just life.

When a mom talks about fatigue and shuttling kids back and forth to a swim meet–moms get it (instantly). We go into thankful prayer and say – "Thank you God for letting me know I'm not alone."

Four years ago, I had a falling out with a dear friend and it hurt like a man stole my money and left me for dead. It was hard to comprehend the end of a friendship. At that moment, all I knew was my heart was broken–we shared everything until I became a mom.

Yes–words were exchanged, things said were probably real wack on my part (since I was going through PPD), and at that moment I felt like I would never get over the ending of the friendship. Guess what? I did.

Now I have a group of supportive mothers and sisters in my circle that share authentically my world of chaos, drama, stress, love, struggle, reinvention and excitement.

The days of being carefree are gone for now; it's the PTA, after-school activities, marriage/relationship, career issues, and 'me' time who has the energy for casual friendships?

I went to the movies with my Mocha Moms, a support group for mothers of color. It was just us savoring a few hours of leaving the house and being simply "Karen," "Rita," "Shannon," "Jay," "Cheryl" and "Diane"–simply a person and not so and so mom.

Remember, your friendship does change with motherhood, however, it does get better when you find the right circle that fits like a good bra.

Understand and Recognize Mom's Silent Killer

I received a few calls/emails about Post Partum Depression (PPD).
PPD is a clinical depression usually affecting women right after childbirth and can last anywhere from a few months to years and can be at the core scary.

This BNM had a 5 month old and said she found the website/blog and felt like she had to call, however, she was not Black.

I thanked her for calling and happily expressed to her that BNM is not solely for Black women; it's a site for all women seeking to renew and redefine their brand post childbirth by any means necessary. I am a Black woman so I pull from my experiences.

I over-stand PPD and experienced it when Sofia was a mere 6 days old. I was not treated with medication, however, the anxiety, depression, and panic attacks did stop at my door and sat in the driver seat for the first year until I battled back and got help with Mocha Moms (my husband gave me the information and I called a year later).

I will say the saving grace was holding my child and breastfeeding everyday, this bond kept me semi-sane and hopeful.

TBNM was created out of my post partum healing and has helped me become empowered each day. I discovered my true voice and passion – helping women to brand self better than before. Amen!

What makes PPD so scary is it effects most women who have defined self via their career, lifestyle and the disease makes you feel insecure, out-of-touch, lost and detached. Not sexy, huh? I lost many friends/opportunities with PPD, you really don't know how to express what you are feeling and leaving the house is a real TASK—so folks give up on you.

To all the BNM suffering...you are not alone. I empower you to discover the strength to get stronger everyday and NEVER give up.

BNM, if you are having unhealthy thoughts and feel like everyone is against you, get help. Seeking professional help through a support group or therapist is one of the most empowering decisions I made to get self back on course. Moms are human with real emotions.

HERE ARE MY TIPS TO REGAIN/RECLAIM SELF:
- Recognize and understand you have PPD.
- Pray for guidance and strength.
- Take baby steps; walk to the corner, leave the house, hold your baby for a few seconds more each day.
- Talk. You must let someone into the darkness—husband/partner/relative/therapist/friend.
- Make your mind up; It's your business to commit to getting better and off medication (if prescribed). You can beat this with W-I-L-L!
- Yoga. It will save and allow you to dig deep within.
- No judgments. Stop beating yourself up.
- Meditate on a time/period you felt powerful and in-charge AND each time you get anxious remember you are a BAD SISTER.
- Stop by *TheBrandNewMommy.com*; we are all sisters in MOTHERHOOD.
- Say this prayer everyday and journal as often as you can to release your fears and create new beginnings.

Healing: Believe in your heart – not your mind.

Know you deserve a fresh start.

Have the power to trust.

Recognize the mind is powerful; however, heart (guts) can be the deciding factor when you want to WIN.

Release yourself today, extend your arms, close your eyes, and release all of your expectations and turn it over to a higher power.

With faith is CONFIDENCE. BELIEF. GUTS.

Trust self and know God will give you more when you realize you DESERVE better.

Source: http://en.wikipedia.org/wiki/Postpartum_depression

Mommy Back to School Tips

Moms spend every day, all year, taking care of others and often times forgetting about their personal brand/self.

Well, it's time to celebrate moms and moms-to-be, especially with the children (almost) back-to-school, here are ways to celebrate the 'brand' new mommy in all of us and attempt a stress-free day:

- **Celebrate your serenity.** Take a trip to a mommy-friendly spa with girlfriends or channel solo power by visiting local spas.
- **Get Naked.** The house is quiet and empty – get into your birthday suit and SCREAM your brains out. You deserve to celebrate self!
- **Get Quiet.** Commit to spending 15 minutes with self and listen to your heart. It's your time to shine.
- **Write it down.** Spend the first day with the kids back to school to write your fall reinvention campaign. What do you want to do? How will you accomplish it? Whom do you need to help achieve it?
- **Get social.** Log onto *livingsocial.com, bestdeals.com* and find the best recession buster treats for your town from dinners to spas, shopping, date night and teeth whitening. Remember, it's all about renewing your personal brand.
- **Get moving.** Purchase a day pass at a gym and come out of your comfort zone with Zumba, Yoga, pilates for $10.00 at the local YMCA.
- **Time for popcorn.** Most cinemas will offer Ladies Day where you can purchase a ticket for $6.50 to see a first run movie and get some alone time.
- **Babysitter, 911!** Hire a babysitter at *www.sitter.com* (this company does the background check) for a few hours to get some alone time.
- **Cocktails!** Ever heard of mommy medicine?

Paula Patton Talk Lip Gloss

In 2011, I met actress and mom, Paula Patton at the Blogalicious Conference in Washington, DC.

I attended the conference since I was new to the blog and vlog scene and wanted to be around moms, women and entrepreneurs reinventing on their terms. The conference was exactly what I needed, a dose of Paula Patton.

Paula Patton was radiant, sweet and shared some tips on the importance of loving self and enjoying the blessing of motherhood. Paula said, "Stay in the mood and moment right now–it's going to be okay."

She stressed not waiting for the perfect moment, simply understanding and embracing your joy while your baby is still a baby.

PAULA PATTON'S TIPS TO ENJOYING MOTHERHOOD:
- Love self no matter what.
- Give energy to your baby, it's a gift.
- Love your partner for who they are not what you want them to be.
- Exercise. Regardless of how you feel, walk 5x a week.
- Commit to feeling good about your inner soul.
- Wear makeup everyday. It can be as simple as lip gloss.
- Dance. Pump up the music and let it all go.
- Get sleep.
- Look and feel cute every chance you get.

Motherhood the Second Time Around at 40

Is there a Dr. in the house?

She is tall, statuesque, beautiful, 45, married for 17 years with a couple of grown kids (respectively 22, 31) and now embracing motherhood a second time around to Leila, almost 4 years old.

This sister needs a medic and a glass of wine stat!

"The newness of being a 'brand' new mom has worn off. I truly love my life and baby but I miss making power deals," says Berenice Mabrey, CEO of Precise Management based in Nashville, TN.

Berenice laughs and says, "It was a gift to give my husband a baby with his DNA—he has been raising mine and now they are all grown up. It's a dream to watch him with our baby, but can a sister get some cardiac resuscitation and conjure up her former life?

She says there are many times when she is gasping for air and feels like the moment won't pass. Berenice is not alone in feeling this way—how many of us can honestly say that motherhood is everything you thought especially when your "career brand" is put on serious HOLD UP, and you are in your 40's? Can you say anxiety?

Sister Berenice, we all feel this way (at some point), so don't beat up yourself. I applaud you for being honest and authentic. Many of us pretend all is well and its not.

As a BNM, your heart will go racing when you remember how fabulous your pre-baby life was—no PR spin here–just hang in there.

Remember, this too shall pass and the baby does grow each moment and you will re-define your brand and become smarter than before. It's much easier for me now with my kids respectively 5 and 13; but I darn sure remember when I too needed cardiac resuscitation. Who am I kidding...I still have those moments albeit fewer.

Motherhood at any age is a precious gift; I've learned that staying in the moment and offering the confusion to a higher power is the best remedy to manage a 'brand' new life. Unfortunately, there is not a mommy manual with solutions for restoring a tired spirit—all we can do is breathe.

HERE IS WHAT CONTINUES TO WORK FOR MANY BNMS:
- Taking routine walks with the baby and breathe.
- Exercise and yoga will save you and reduce stress.
- Daycare/nanny care is imperative—even if its just for 2 -3 hours.
- Do something exclusively for you once a week.
- Sleep every chance you get.
- Make love to your husband and channel that inner sexy.
- Join a support group, 'cause you are not alone—I love Mocha Moms.
- Wine. That's good mommy medicine after the kids have gone to bed. No drinking and driving.
- Pray and pray.
- Enjoy your gift; many people try to conceive each day.

BNM Note: We do not judge in this space called *TheBrandNewMommy.com*.

Mothers are not perfect–we are all work in progress…especially us Career Moms on hiatus.

ACT II : BRANDING

You are a brand!

The impression that you are giving off right now to your kids, family, co-workers, and strangers is your personal brand.

A brand is a consistent experience someone encounters every time they interact with you. Think of it like McDonalds french fries, it always tastes the same no matter what.

ACT II : BRANDING

3 Power Ways to Kickoff your Style with Kimora Lee Simmons

Kimora Lee Simmons is all about the business and multiple streams of income.

Let's learn a few tips from KLS for 2013!

Savvy businesswoman, author, philanthropist, producer, top model, television personality, Tony-Award winner and—according to *Forbes* Magazine—Kimora Lee Simmons is one of the top "hardest working mothers in Hollywood."

Her vivacious personality and stunning beauty are familiar around the world, but these attributes only scratch the surface of one of the most dynamic and influential businesswomen in fashion and entertainment. Kimora Lee Simmons has accomplished what many may not accomplish in a lifetime.

HERE IS WHAT I LEARNED FROM KIMORA LEE SIMMONS ON HOW TO MAKE 2013 THE BEST 'BRAND' NEW YEAR!

- **Be you authentically!** Enough said.
- **Embrace change.** Manage the ups and downs of your lifestyle (divorce, career, stress, family) with class.
- **Upgrade your style for 2012!** Define your signature look and work it like a rock-star.
- **Diversify your business portfolio.** Create an international marketing/pr plan for your business/brand and go for it. Think huge and don't be afraid to put your face on the product.
- **Empower the next generation of entrepreneurs.** It's important to groom our children—teach them everything and make certain they understand the business.
- **Claim it fiscally!** It's not how you start; it's what you do with the knowledge you have. Start to make changes towards a better life financially.

Five Ways to Stay Mentally Charged!

Mental Health is everything.
Your mental acumen, sharpness, bold vision and perception of the world will impact your outcome—good or bad. Really, it's up to you and that's what I've learned.

I own so many self-help/motivational books that I can start a wing at any library; and, all the books have a universal message—control your thoughts and you will control your outcome.

As entrepreneurs/brand new mommas/talented peeps, you've got to channel the positivity even when you don't feel like it.

What you think is what you attract. It's amazing how my mind can create drama and my body responds as if it was programmed. Deepness!

The next time you start to think negatively, shut it down and say, "I'm not buying what you are selling today, visit someone else!"

5 WAYS TO STAY MENTALLY HEALTHY
- Prayer and Meditation.
- Authenticity. Be you and tell the truth.
- Stop striving for perfection, it's doesn't exist.
- Don't judge. Your scale of excellence is just that, your scale.
- Love your reflection.
- Shut the crap down immediately when it enters your mind.

Karen, the brand new mommy is a work-in-progress, strives to be authentic by simply nurturing her mind, body and soul; and, works diligently at keeping haters at bay.

Seven Tips To Marketing Your Authentic Self

Have you ever thought of getting paid for all the professional advice you dish out to professional colleagues, family and friends?

A professional speaker is one who connects with their audience, while sharing their skills and showcasing their authenticity and expertise on a subject matter.

Although it may sound lucrative, a career as a professional speaker will require work, time, money, and possibly a booking agent.

"One becomes a professional expert speaker when they create content with outstanding platform skills (connecting with the audience)," says Norma Hollis, a professional speaker strategist and CEO of **Norma Thompson Hollis Inc.** To be a successful speaker, Hollis adds you should offer the following: know and be comfortable with your authentic voice and always deliver good and memorable content.

Becoming an expert speaker is a strategic opportunity to leverage/enhance your brand. Each time you connect with your audience, which will ultimately elevate business persona and provide free advertising via impressions to a wider audience. "It provides one with more exposure, additional revenue, and an opportunity to showcase their magic by taking a boring topic and transforming it into one of extreme engagement," says Hollis.

Expert status as a speaker does not happen overnight. Hollis' company offers authentic development training services/workshops for speakers; message development coaching; and marketing services to assist clients with securing paid bookings for their respective topic/passion. She also runs a speakers agency that books professional speakers.

Keep in mind that a legitimate speakers agency will charge an upfront fee for their services. Most agencies will ask you to pay a monthly retainer and an agreed commission for confirmed speaking engagements.

BNM, if you are interested in becoming a professional speaker then take the time to create, develop, and grow your brand. The best way to test the market with your message and style is to join local organizations such as Toastmasters International and the Chamber of Commerce. Practice your message at the meetings while receiving valuable feedback/critiques from experts.

> **NORMA HOLLIS' TIPS TO BECOMING AN EXPERT SPEAKER:**
> - Know your message.
> - Tap into your experience, expertise, and passion.
> - Know and be your authentic self at all times.
> - Listen to your inner voice.
> - Be clear on your values.
> - Know and use your experience to motivate others.
> - Treat self as a brand and negotiate wisely.

9 Steps for Working Smoothly With Friends and Family

Entrepreneurship is not an easy game—especially during an economic downturn.

Most entrepreneurs are looking for a way to be strategic with their funds, and, most times that involves bartering, and hoping for a hookup from family and friends.

I am no different when it comes to looking for a hookup—especially when your husband is an award-winning graphic designer and chief idea maker for Straight Design.

Recently, I hired my husband to create a logo for my new venture—The Brand New Mommy, the ultimate destination for savvy Black women seeking to renew and redefine their personal brand post childbirth. Who better to hire than someone who understands and has witnessed my struggle first hand?

For the past six months I've been writing about authenticity and the importance of the big "reveal." Well, this business relationship with my husband was less than ideal. I was not pleased with the way he handled the project, which led to a tense household for many days.

"Family members always feel they have limitless entitlement and no boundaries simply because there is a personal connection," said my husband Andrew Bass after days of heated discord.

In previous posts I've stressed the importance of branding and how the logo is the artery of the company, especially when launching a brand in a competitive digital age. My husband created 5-6 concepts for TBNM and the first five did not hit the mark. After several heated creative meetings, debriefs, and attitudes—I received a concept that captured the essence of the brand new mommy.

How do you move past the "personal" feelings and ensure that the next "working" experience will be better? Andrew says, "Both parties should create a realistic checklist of what is expected and the time-frame to accomplish the project. Most importantly, offer some form of monetary compensation—immediate or deferred—so that no one feels compromised."

There is an often mistaken assumption that entrepreneurs are cheap and always looking for a "favor." Not exactly—entrepreneurs want the best as the next competitive business owner and, yes, we do prefer to hire family/friends because ultimately they believe in us and there is trust.

HERE ARE MY NINE TIPS WHEN CONSIDERING WORKING WITH FAMILY/FRIENDS:
- Ask questions (first). Have a to-do list of what you want to accomplish and listen to hear if they have time for your project.
- Offer compensation for services. It's best to agree on an exact dollar amount and get it in writing.
- Refer a business lead. Everyone can use your family/friend talent—why not talk him or her up.
- Sign a contract and get the terms in writing. Protect your household and relationships.
- Conduct business during office hours only.
- Set meetings outside of the home.
- Manage expectations.
- Check your tone. It's not what you say; it's how you say it.
- Be appreciative of the service.

9 Tips to Becoming the Next Terry McMillan

Are you a novelist waiting to exhale? If so, it is time to make your passion a reality. Terry McMillan made it happen and so can you.

Meet Faye Thompson, a government employee for more than 25 years whose recent novel is being compared to Terry McMillan's *Disappearing Acts*. Thompson's second novel, *Cheesecake and Teardrops* (Urban Trade Paper, $12.95), was written during her lunch hour, vacation, weekend, after hours—basically any time she wasn't at her 9-to-5 job.

"I wanted to write and tell a story that I could not stop reading. If it's your passion, find the time to do it," says Thompson. "Get your hands on the Literary Marketplace, a [compendium] of agents, publishers, and editors. This resource will show you how to submit materials/manuscripts the right way. Also, take a creative writing course offered at a local college. This will empower you to tap into your power," advises Thompson.

Sometimes the upfront cost for pursuing your passion can just be time and discipline. "I scored my book deal by networking and going to book signings and talking to the authors. Word of mouth is powerful—and preparation is even better. New authors must make it their business to promote and understand that they are a brand in progress," says Thompson.

FAYE THOMPSON'S TIPS TO BECOMING A BEST-SELLING AUTHOR:

- **Do your research.** Use the free resources available at your local library to research your topic and keep costs to a minimum.
- **Stay focused.** Keep your eye on your ultimate goal.
- **Be patient.** Don't be discouraged if your rewards don't happen immediately.
- **Listen to your inner voice and trust your instincts.** When in doubt, go with your gut.
- **Don't edit self.** At least not when writing the first draft. Get everything on paper or your computer screen before you start refining your story.

- **Let it flow.** Write, write, write. And then write some more.
- **Have fun with characters/story.** If you're bored by your story, odds are readers will be too.
- **Self-promote.** Send out your press kit, talk yourself up, start a website, blog, create a social media strategy to publicize your brand.
- **Network.** Go out and meet other authors, publishers, and editors.

I empower you to dust off the noggin and write a best seller as you self-publish or score a publishing deal, and channel your inner passion.

10 Tips for Writing a Winning E-Book

Would you like to solidify your expert status in your respective field, score another stream of income, and promote your business? It's time to get published and write an e-book.

With the advent of technology—we crave information immediately, passionately and succinctly. An electronic or e-book allows you to become a self-published author and add your innovative approach to a topic within 7 to 10 days.

The great news is writing an e-book requires very little commitment. No need to purchase any pricey software—MS Word or other word processing software is suitable, and, you can complete your book in a weekend. The e-book can be as few as 5 pages and no more than 50. A great guide on completing an e-book is *How to Write and Publish Your Own e-Book in as Little as 7 Days* (Morgan James Publishing;$19.95).

The key to writing a winning e-book is that it must be informative, engaging, be of service, and offer a new spin on what's already out in the marketplace.

When you are ready to write your e-book, start with an outline—think about what you do best—legal advice, cooking, haircare, human resource retention, marketing, finance, public relations, dating, etc and then start researching. Next write ten things you would offer in your book for the readers that would be considered "must" have information and resources.

TIPS TO GET YOU STARTED:

- **Identify your topic/genre with thought.** Think about how you can be of service with your expertise and say a different way to entice readers.
- **Come up with a catchy title to seduce readers.** The title should convey information about the e-book.
- **Write short introductions about the content** of the book in the table of contents for your readers to glean what they will learn from your presentation.

- **Know your audience.** Tailor the information to their liking, add anecdotes to personalize, and avoid the SAT vocabulary words. Keep it simple.
- **Hire a graphic designer.** The designer will create an attractive cover for the e-book, which will make your product competitive.
- **Proofread the document.** Ask your family and friends to look it over for grammar and spelling.
- **Make it personal.** If you can add photos, data and stats it will make your book more marketable.
- **Convert your final document to a PDF file.** A PDF file makes it challenging for others to copy your book, and the documents are easily transmitted via email and downloads for purchase.
- **Pricing is key.** Do your research and make certain that your ask is competitive.
- **Market yourself.** Sell your e-book on your website, blog, social media sites and professional organizations.

A Polished Image Improves Brand Confidence

According to image expert Wadlington, a polished look "depends on industry and environment."

For the past few weeks I have been struggling with my hair.

I know, that old saw of black women and our hair, when will it end? As you can see from my photo, I wear my hair natural. But as I continue on this path of re-invention, I was in a quandary over how best to present a polished image. Is my natural hair projecting a polished image along with my wardrobe?

A polished image is defined as a well-put together style, which reflects and captures the essence of who you are with confidence and grace. It means dressing appropriately for the right environment and having a professional appearance.

People only see the packaging and if that's not together you (may) have lost the opportunity before you've had a chance to open your mouth and sell yourself. Regardless of the field you are in, appearance matters, especially, if you're a woman. You must consider everything from your shoes to your hair and anything in between—including your briefcase and/or handbag to capture that winning look.

Along with the hair drama for women, the wardrobe factor can become tricky when creating the "power" look each time you step outside for work, after work, an interview, or a formal event. Men have it easy, regardless of the time of day, their wardrobe choices are quite basic: slacks, jacket, tie, crisp white shirt, and a polished shoe.

"A well-conceived image from head to toe is a polished look, and that all depends on industry and environment," says Cheryl Ann Wadlington, creative director of Evoluer Image Consultants. "If you were in a creative field it would be different from a law firm. In corporate America you wear traditional clothes—a crisp white shirt, pair of slacks, closed toe shoe with no detail, pearl earrings....Confidence and know-how are important but appearance matters more."

Being your true authentic self is important, but there is a time and place. Once you've secured the opportunity, de-code the corporate culture, and then and only then should you incorporate your personal style into the job. How you market yourself for the position is key and you will want to keep a consistent image.

Wadlington passionately explains, "Brand confidence is how you speak, walk, talk, dress, attitude – all has to be packaged with the look from head to toe."

A POLISHED IMAGE COUPLED WITH BRAND CONFIDENCE EQUALS THE ABILITY TO TAKE CHARGE AND OWN A SITUATION:

- Dress the part and look fabulous.
- Know the dress code of the company and if you don't know it, ask.
- Neat hair is a must, whether you have dreadlocks, chemical relaxer or a weave.
- Choose your underpinnings (underwear, bra) wisely. Pull up the "girlies," and make sure you're wearing a proper fitting bra. "Eight out of ten women wear an incorrect bra and should be fitted by an expert," says Wadlington.
- All professional women should have a quality and classic handbag. It doesn't have to be expensive, but it shouldn't be cheap.
- Don't go overboard with the jewelry. Invest in a quality watch to accessorize the outfit.

Blueprint for Success

While January is usually the best time to dust off and prepare to win for a new start, any month is just as good. Regardless of what was, it's just that–WAS (wasting away sulking).

This year is a chance to be better, smarter, prouder, stronger, and take no mess.

The best way to kick off my blog about branding, entrepreneurism, and marketing for Women of Power is to offer you inspiration and a "business" game plan offered by my mentor, Beverly Kearney, University of Texas (Austin), track and field superstar coach, former All-American, and philanthropist, to set off 2010.

But who am I to offer advice? Proudly and emphatically, I am Karen Taylor Bass, the PR Expert, author, radio host, motivational speaker, and "brand" new mommy. I have spent 20 years as a media strategist/marketing expert/media coach for corporations such as: Sony Music, Coca-Cola, United Negro College Fund, Harper Collins, and EMI to name a few. I am the public relations expert who helped change the landscape of urban music in the '90s with the neo-soul movement. Now I am a proud entrepreneur holding strong in the midst of an economic tsunami. I retired from corporate America several years ago upon getting married and having an instant family.

Coach Bev shared how she was chosen by a higher power to live after a near fatal car accident. The doctors told her to prepare to die. Her chance for a full recovery was bleak--she was paralyzed, faced multiple surgeries, and had a narrow chance of ever coaching her team to another NCAA title. When told of her prognosis, Coach Bev said she looked the team of doctors in the face and replied, "Are you kidding me? My faith is strong and I'm not ready to die. I have overcome more than this. Giving up is failing, which is not an option for me at any time." (Listen to our uplifting interview and discussion, *www.blogtalkradio.com/theprexpert.com*.)

It never crossed Coach Bev's mind that she was not going to make a full recovery. I wonder how many of us have that feeling of determination to go the distance with our "business" game plan?

How many of us have thought about giving up on our dreams, business, and most importantly self? I know I have.

A true champion is taught that, in life, there is only one option—winning.

Let's not wait to be given a dire prognosis. Decide today to create a bold, winning game plan for this year and beyond.

HERE IS COACH BEV'S BLUEPRINT FOR SUCCESS:

- **Do something different for better results.** Only a fool would continue to do business the same way they did in 20012 and expect to win in 2013.
- **Know your desired outcome.** If that outcome is to WIN, then use the most strategic and smartest approach to WIN (big). There are no rules. Create your own.
- **Don't be afraid to fail.** Failure allows you to rethink your strategy in order to grow. Never allow a failure to get you stuck. Remember—it's all part of the process.
- **Speak it.** If you believe you are the best-then shout it from the mountain top and let it be recorded and heard. You have to be your own cheerleader, and make certain to travel in a sphere of greatness.
- **Take action now.** There's no time to say, "shoulda, coulda, woulda"—that's so 2009. You want to change your lot in life, well put one foot in front of the other and get to it. Action yields results.
- **Go for the gold.** Yes, we are in a recession. However, someone is getting business and why shouldn't it be you? Let decision makers know that you are open for strategic business, joint ventures, and international travel. Take the road less traveled and beat your competition and stand out.

Are you ready to show and prove? What is your life/career challenge?

Brand Age: Lessons to Learn from Demi Moore

In a society where the images of timeless youth, beauty and weight take center stage daily what's an aging momma to do?

Demi Moore seemed to have it all–family, fame, fortune and fans, however, it was not enough.

The aging process is not fun. As I prepare to turn 45 years YOUNG in March, I've experienced the challenges of getting older.

Let's just say I am adjusting to a few tweaks; I now wear readers (granny glasses) to read the fine print, battled with sciatica for 4 weeks in December, and, when it rains I can feel a touch of arthritis. Sound sexy yet?

Surely I get caught up from time to time with the basic beauty s!#t because I might feel insecure that day or week, but when that happens I take a personal timeout and love up on my self, indulge in family and friends.

I understand Demi's issue with age and dealing with life scandals in the public eye as a former entertainment publicist. Egos are fragile especially when your life is on constant blast; however, it's time for Demi to pull it together.

As women we must believe/know that we are enough—regardless of what's going on externally with life circumstances. At the BET Honors, Dr. Maya Angelou said, "Love your truth."

What I learned from Demi Moore's tragedy is that I am more than enough and getting older will be okay if I continue to love the person in the mirror looking back at me.

LESSONS TO LEARN FROM DEMI MOORE:
- Define your standard of beauty first. If you truly believe that you are a dime piece hold on tight.
- Act your age at all times.
- Parent your children; you had your glory days already.

Brush Off Your Old Way of Thinking

It's no secret that given the economy, it is imperative to market your best self when seeking clients, employment opportunities, and growing a business. In an unsettled economy, everyone must develop a new attitude to stand out from the competition, and the time to start is today, as we welcome love me day!

I have put together a PR Re-Invention Plan to help business owners and individuals secure the opportunity they desire using PR as an empowerment tool. (Just so we're all on the same page, I define re-invention as a transformation into the life you've always craved.) Keep in mind these tips have worked for my past clients, including Citibank, Sony Music, recording artists D'Angelo and Jill Scott, and the NBA's Ray Allen and Chris Webber.

Re-invention will not be easy; however, if you come up with a plan, stick with it, and you can have truly substantial returns.

Here are some sure-fire ways to spring forward your brand, market your business, and stand out—all on a budget.

Think linearly. Act with a plan. Identify where you want to work, what salary you want to make, and how you can be of value to a corporation on your terms. Create a strategy to achieve those goals.

Use social media. The Internet is a force and you must participate. For companies and clients to find you, participate in social networking. Blog, create a podcast, send e-newsletters, and star in your own viral video. It is imperative to have a Web presence with a functional, smart, attractive Website.

Be prepared for opportunity. Let people know what you have to offer. Be your own publicist and bring the hype. Create an electronic media kit listing your skills, accomplishments, and awards. Make certain your presentation is creative and appropriate for your industry.

Polish your image. Make sure that you're you projecting the message you want people to see? Ask your friends, family members, and colleagues of their impressions of you.

Self-promotion isn't a bad thing. You are an authority in your field so begin to visualize and execute your plan as if you were a rock star. Write an Op-Ed for your favorite newspaper, contribute to a blog, or secure a byline (this means that you get credit for writing the story). Service the byline to the companies you want to work for and stay on their radar.

Be confident. If you say you are the best—then bring it. Show letters of recommendations, praises from your former boss/project managers, and colleagues. Remember, you are entitled to success.

Tap into your network to increase your net worth. It is imperative that you keep in touch with past co-workers. Your contacts can lead you to a contract, job opportunities, meetings, and leads, which can eventually increase your bottom line.

Get a mentor. Make certain that the mentor you choose has time to be a mentor. Be clear about expectations and time and make it a two-way street.

Give back. A great deal of business is done while volunteering, which can provide you a legitimate aura of leadership, dedication, and commitment.

Is this 'Brand' new mommy stuck?

Have you ever felt stuck in an image time warp?

Every time you reconnect with someone from your past they say, "Wow, you look exactly the same, recognized your hairstyle a mile away."

Hmmm.

Then you start to think and feel some kinda way, prompting you to go through photos from the past twenty plus years and realize damn—I've only had a variation of the same look for a long long time.

Am I stuck?

I went natural at age 25, and never really looked back except for a perm here and there for a major event - my wedding and life changes.

A friend of mine recently told me she got a perm after 15 years of having dreadlocks and couldn't believe how she is treated differently with her new blond weave. It seems the 'new' brand is loved by all and she gets upgraded at the airport, hotel, business is booming, etc. Really?

I'm beginning to think my natural style is stale and it might be time to get a cute little pixie to usher in some brand new change I'm always professing?

Don't get me wrong, I love my hair and have had EVERY possible natural style: bald, locks, twist, afro, mohawk, and braids, perhaps, it's time to get a new look?

How important is hair and can a 'new' style transcend one's brand to the next level?

Since we share so much, this time is no different.

Lessons Learned from "Brand' J-Hudson

Kudos to Jennifer Hudson!
She is talented, beautiful, smart, strategic, skinny, grounded and a cover girl.

Recently, I received my *Ebony* magazine with the svelte 'brand' new mommy on the cover. Let me just say—*Ebony* is really looking good and I'm feeling it all over again. You?

How many times have you divinely avoided a near-death experience by following your gut and said, "Wow, that could have been me?"

The J-Hud article really speaks to divine intuition; when you get that uncanny twinge, listen and follow that feeling.

As I read the article, Jennifer, shared how she was supposed to be in Chicago during the brutal murders of her mother, brother and nephew; however, she went to support her fiancé David Otunga at a wrestling match in Tampa instead. Can you say DIVINE intervention?

HERE IS WHAT I KNOW WE CAN LEARN FROM JENNIFER HUDSON:
- **Prayer up!** Laugh if you want but prayer and faith really does work. Timing is everything. No need to fret, what is divinely yours is yours.
- **Brand you!** Tribulations will come and go, stay steadfast, work on your brand consistently and be ready for the opportunity.
- **Reinvent.** You can go from a cashier at McDonalds to American Idol contestant, Academy Award winner, mother, and Weight Watchers brand ambassador and now author.
- **Dream gargantuan.** When you believe in possibilities, outrageous blessings (will) happen.

Do you believe in divine intervention?

# Jumpstarting Your Personal Brand After Mommy-hood

Mommy-hood is no easy feat; regardless of age your mind, body, spirit and career will never be the same. The moment you meet your healthy and beautiful bundle of joy, your priorities will shift and you will change.

But after the maternity leave has ended, how do you re-invent your personal brand to incorporate your new status when its time to go back to work?

At 43, with two kids (including a toddler), and in the midst of a re-invention, I have recently upgraded from sweatpants to fitted jeans, and the process to become the "brand" new mommy has not been easy. I had a thought: do all mommies—including celebrities—struggle to *re-define* their personal brand? The answer is a resounding yes.

I spoke with Grammy Award winning artist Monica, about re-defining her brand after a brief hiatus from the music industry. Sure, she has "fame," a TV show, and a new album coming out, but at the end of the day, she shares the same concerns as I do about re-invention and re-entering the workforce after becoming a parent.

"The best sage wisdom someone told me about re-invention is to focus on the positive, what makes you special and different, and realize that just because you put yourself first, doesn't mean your kids are not your first concern," said the single mother of two pre-schoolers. Re-invention is not about the superficial but the qualities that make you feel centered as a person, says Monica.

After taking time off to have her children, Monica is back with a vengeance. She has a reality show on BET that chronicles her re-invention as she finds balance being a single parent, dealing with high blood pressure, recording a new album, building a business, and struggling to carve out moments to be still. Her fifth album, "Still Standing," is scheduled for release on March 23. She chose the name as a testament of strength to all of us finding our way back home to self.

"Re-invention happened for me organically and I learned that it can't be contrived," she says. "My oldest son, Ramone, almost 5, loves to hear me sing and perform; he was the one that encouraged me to get back out there. I started this journey at 14 and built over 15 years of relationship. Re-invention is not about working hard, it's about being smarter, utilizing and preserving relationships, and having a dynamite support system [mom, aunt, and cousins]. Pay attention to your elders and shape shift your mommy-hood to work for you."

Listening to her, I realized that Monica is wise beyond her 29 years.

The same way it is important to refresh our brand and skills to take advantage of a job or opportunity during this recession, it is as important, if not crucial to renew and redefine the personal brand upon giving birth. It is imperative that we do not lose our magic once we have children.

"When you re-invent allow your brand to speak for itself, take your time and feel pretty—pray, light candles, walk, and remember you are the most important person. Re-invention is about weathering the storm, claiming victory, being comfortable in one's skin and making no apologies. That's what re-invention and mommy-hood are all about," says Monica.

I learned that regardless of age, socioeconomic status, and career choice, there is no quick fix for re-invention when it comes to mommies.

MONICA'S RE-INVENTION TIPS FOR WOMEN:

- **Be Faithful.** Spirituality is key and will play a major role in life. Don't fight it; just accept the fact that you are not in control.
- **Prioritize.** Your kids and family comes first.
- **De-clutter.** Negativity becomes a hindrance. Clear out things that no longer work—be they relationships, jobs, or items from your past.
- **Respect Yourself.** Don't sell yourself short for anyone or any opportunity.
- **Ownership is Key.** You are your own boss, act and do what you want to do, when you want to do it.
- **Assemble an A-Team.** Your support system and relationships are key ingredients for re-invention. Conjure up the female power. Join a support group like Mocha Moms.

Mentorship Is as Important as Oxygen

As you pound the pavement and scour the Internet in search of a job, client or opportunity—an important task to add to your to-do list for career advancement is securing a mentor.

While the job landscape has changed with the advent of social media, what a mentor does has not. A mentor is still someone who has specific skills, knowledge and abilities to help groom you for success, provides strategic business advice and assists you with the tools to negotiate and conquer the corporate terrain. A mentor can be especially helpful for women who have the two-fold challenge of navigating the sexism of the business world while still maintaining a home and children. Choosing the right mentor will help maintain sanity as you climb the ladder.

"For African Americans mentoring is like oxygen; mentorship helps one uncover the opportunities and possibilities that are beyond the stratosphere," says Kimberly Reed, human resource consultant and managing partner of The Reed Development Group.

A successful mentor will be compatible to her mentee, accomplished, connected, and available, and someone who also uses an innovative approach to maneuver the politics and drama of the corporate world. With mentoring you can achieve the following: creating a blueprint for your long-term career goal; securing invitations for the "right" networking functions; mastering the art of negotiation; and winning tips to climbing the corporate ladder.

"Mentoring is coming from an authentic place of service and pouring into an individual the necessary tools [etiquette/protocol, networking, strategic alliances, wellness and career coaching] for winning in a male-dominated world and a near-to-invisible culture for women," says Carol Harvey, mentor advocate for Delta Sigma Theta sorority (Philadelphia chapter), and manager of admissions for Thomas Jefferson University Hospital.

A mentoring relationship is not just a one-way street. You, as the mentee, must play a strategic and proactive role in their professional development, according to the

Department of Health and Human Services. The agency goes on to say that in order to take full advantage of a mentor/mentee relationship, a mentee must be open to feedback and coaching.

"Mentorship is a developmental relationship, says Ella L.J. Edmondson Bell, Ph.D., founder and president of ASCENT-Leading Multicultural Women to the Top, and author of *Career GPS: Strategies for Women Navigating the New Corporate Landscape* (Amistad; $25.99). "It's a dance. It's like any other kind of relationship; you have to get to know someone. The mentor shares his or her wisdom and knowledge. You share your perception of what's happening in your company from your level. Look for mentors around you. You need allies, colleagues, and peers. Mentors are supposed to support you. That support is circular, not linear."

As women we must openly celebrate each other, formulate healthy networks and relationships. It is critical to have a mentor, however, it is crucial to give back and become a mentor. To get involved today, check out *www.caresmentoring.com*.

According to HHS, a mentor should possess:

- *Strong interpersonal skills*
- *Organizational knowledge*
- *Technical competence*
- *Strong leadership skills*
- *Sense of personal power*
- *Ability to maintain confidentiality of mentoring relationship*
- *Willingness to be supportive and patient*

Is Your Brand Bold, Beautiful, & Determined?

It may be trite but it is very true; First impressions are everything.
Branding is an overused word. How do you create the perfect brand - in life and in business? By being a bold dreamer?

Branding is simply a consistent feeling, image, and experience desired from a product conveyed to the general public. Basically, you—the entrepreneur—are the brand. The minute someone interfaces with you, they are deciding if they should do business with your brand based on their perception of you. Is your message big, bold, and beautiful?

Over time, we all go through brand re-invention (strategizing, tweaking, and shedding), hopefully becoming mo' better. While watching the Golden Globe Awards in January and seeing the re-invention of Brand Mo'Nique, I was truly inspired by her authenticity.

She has shown her versatility since the beginning of her career. From stand-up comedian, to wisecracking actress, author, producer, late-night host, and now Oscar-nominated actress. Her passion has remained steady and consistent with her best-selling book, *Skinny Women Are Evil: Notes of a Big Girl in a Small-Minded World*, even as she (now) approaches a more svelte model of herself. Brand Mo'Nique has never wavered on authenticity; she simply made adjustments along the way—while playing by her rules.

Monique is a great symbol of what it means to be a dreamer. Dreams should be big, bold, and beautiful. In a recent acceptance speech, Mo'Nique talked about being 14 years old and dreaming of becoming a star. Her speech underscores what I have always believed—the bigger the dream, the more successful the brand.

START DREAMING BIG AND BOLD TODAY:
- **Dreams don't happen overnight.** It takes heart, persistence, money, and blessings to make one's dream become a reality.
- **Dreams must be gargantuan.** It's not acceptable to just dream. Your dream must be out of this world so that when you tell people about them—they laugh.

If your peers are not laughing then you are dreaming too small.
- **Dreams only flourish with confidence.** Mo'Nique boldly has set the path of what it means to be bold, bright, and ambitious. Consider this—Mo'Nique refused to participate in the required Hollywood schmooze-fest (in order to secure an Oscar nomination for her role in Precious (based on the Novel *Push* by Sapphire) and still received the nod. It's okay to play by your rules.
- **Dreams must have clarity.** Know what you want, how you want it, and with whom you want it. When you ask, you will receive. Make certain you are asking wisely.
- **Dreams are ordained.** Tap into a higher spirit and simply believe.
- **Dreams have vampires.** Stay away from those who can seek to rob you of your chance/opportunity. Keep the haters at bay.
- **Dream in color.** Mo'Nique saw her moment and now she can actively participate.

Dreaming big is only one step of Brand You.

Positioning Yourself for an Opportunity

Have I told you how fabulous you are lately?

As a fellow entrepreneur, you are not alone in your struggle, stress, and lack of resources for your multi-million dollar corporation. It is a struggle for most given the economy.

With high unemployment among African Americans, now is a great time to become an entrepreneur. Entrepreneurs are passionate, fearless, resourceful, and the driving force of the economy. Regardless of what you have been told, companies are hiring consultants with a fresh winning perspective and a flexible engagement fee; and now is the time to position yourself as an authority in your field, commit to doing something different, and offer your talent/services to multiple (small to midsize) companies to secure consistent business.

Get ready to implement my tips over the next few weeks to build your brand, create a niche, formulate a winning plan, and most importantly secure FREE (do-it-yourself) press. Here are several steps to help separate your brand and mission from the competition.

Are you ready?

You want it so bad...you can taste, drink, and see your success. Is your team in place? Many times people are not prepared for the avalanche of blessings when they occur, please be ready. Here are a few tips to get you started:

- **Be prepared.** Success can smell success. Have that look about you, dress appropriately, and have your message on hand to deliver the pitch and close the deal. If you believe in your product others will come to the party in a matter of time.
- **Reputation is everything.** Let your work and rep speak for you. If you give your word, honor it. Don't commit if you cannot meet deadline—people always remember the screw up.

- **Speak up.** If you don't agree with someone's agenda or how they are positioning your product speak up. Being amenable to everything will not garner fans, only enemies down the line.
- **Be well-rounded.** Make certain that you are knowledgeable about current events; this will empower you to have a conversation with any CEO, mogul, or average Jane.
- **Be proactive.** If there is someone that you want to get in contact with—reach out. Write a letter, send an email, and make a call; look within your circle for a connection. Work in that order and you will get results.
- **Make time for others.** Time is a premium and you are a priority. Make certain that you treat yourself and others that way. If someone is reaching out to you, then you must respond in a timely fashion.
- **Get to know the "team."** Don't be an elitist and ignore the administrative assistant, receptionist, or mailroom clerks. They are the ones really running the company and are privy to information. Be polite and respectful to everyone and become allies with those in the know.
- **Stay out of gossip.** Don't get caught up not minding your business, which means not taking care of your money.
- **Steer clear of dream vampires.** Don't share your dream with people unless they are like-minded and possess the same energy as you.
- **Network and use your connections.** I don't know why we always forget to tap into our database and circle. Join organizations to widen your networking base and utilize your friends/co-workers/affiliation to make the introduction for you.
- **Empower yourself and others.** Give back to others from a sacred space and be counted. You can volunteer, make a contribution or just be there for someone in need.
- **Be consistent.** If you provide service a certain way…continue to provide it that same way, only BETTER.
- **Be viral.** The Internet is a force and you must participate. For companies to prosper they must register with an online social network for connections (LinkedIN, Pinterest Facebook, Twitter); blog; e-blast newsletters; webinars; and podcast.
- **Smile and be engaging.**

Pro Bono Mommy: Stop Giving Away your Expertise

Moms, stop giving away your expertise and talent for free.
The economic landscape is screaming for moms, however, when one of us second-guesses our expertise and decides to give away talent, brain trust, and personality, it devalues the MOM BRAND.

At one time, I was so happy to be included and would have given away the kitchen sink, but FREE can't pay the mortgage or bills. Stop the pro bono.

Pro bono is defined as services done or donated without charge.

Lately, I've been meeting moms who are simply happy to get an invitation/product review while giving away their talents for free. Stop!

We must declare a value on our talent and make it work. What is the compensation needed to share your talent? Not all compensation is monetary; you can also consider the barter agreement when mutually beneficial.

BNM, let's make a covenant that we will only agree to a certain amount of pro bono gigs/opportunities per year.

Motherhood is a sisterhood and we must be one another's keeper. Reinvention is not easy, but we must not forget our talent pre and post motherhood. Starting today, let's determine our worth at fair market value and create the pricing menu for our services.

Start thinking about how you will market your expertise and create a plan of action right now. Remember, baby steps really do count.

Score A-List Public Relations on a Shoestring Budget, Part I

So, how do A-list celebrities and corporations secure that ultimate public relations campaign that has them on everyone's lips?

First, let's talk about what public relations entails: fostering public goodwill and creating a favorable opinion for a product, person, or thing. Basically, it attracts consumer attention to a product and is generally a well-planned campaign. Public relations is not about creating a one-shot hype campaign, planning a special event, and hosting a party for the media. That's called publicity.

Lisa Price of the popular and multimillion-selling natural haircare company Carol's Daughter certainly secures A-list PR now, however, that was not always the case. So what did she do?

She created both short-term and long-term plans, hired top-notch professionals—strategic marketing and brand expert Steve Stoute, along with celebrity endorsers including Will and Jada Pinkett Smith and Mary J. Blige—to promote her brand and business.

Most burgeoning stars and business owners hire a publicist, which can range from $2,500 to $10,000 a month. It is possible to do it yourself, and as the PR expert, I'm going to show you how.

These strategies will not only get you started; they will empower you to win and standout from the competition:

1. **Define your message.** Take the time to write and research what you want to convey. Identify your target audience, your strengths, niche, and specify what you are offering that is different from your competition. It's not always about being the best—it's about being consistent and giving the same experience each time.

2. **Create a logo.** A logo also called the identity is the heart of your company and brand. The identity becomes the face for your brand and it must reflect the essence of what your company represents. While you might think that you

can create a logo yourself, consider that a company can spend hundreds of thousands of dollars to develop just one logo. I suggest using a professional. Visit graphic design organization sites such as AIGA and Graphic Artists Guild.

3. **Disseminate your message appropriately.** What tools will you use to spread your message (press release, biography, blog, etc.)? If you want to get the most out of your budget, start with a press release and a biography (highlights of your success), a well-written biography can range from $500 - $3000. Also, begin to blog about your expertise and offer tips to garner media attention. Monthly press release. This is generally used to announce something new with your company—it can be a product, award, new hire or new client. Press releases typically range from $250-$1000. Black News and National Newspaper Association each cost about $150 and will send out your press release to over 50,000 consumers. NNPA will send your press release to all the national black newspapers (over 270), and it will also send you a PDF of each story that is written about you or your product).

Having an interesting and compelling press release is a sure-fire way to guarantee coverage. My e-Book, *You Want Caviar But Have Money For Chitlins: A Smart Do-It-Yourself PR Guide For Those A Budget* ($13.99) provides step-by-step tips along with a diagram to write an A-List release.

Media meeting. Read and get to know journalists who write about what you're selling. If you like an article they wrote, send them a note, and definitely follow them on social media platforms like Twitter and Facebook. Don't always think about the pitch—get to know them first.

Website. This is your ultimate marketing tool to running a profitable business with an international presence. You will need to hire a Web designer or a Web hosting company to create the site. Visit *www.smallbusiness.yahoo.com* and *www.networksolutions.com*.

Be sure to choose an appropriate domain name. It represents both the Web address of your site and the name visitors will use to refer to your company. Keep in mind that you want to own and purchase your domain name to secure your rights as your brand becomes profitable. Many companies offer competitive pricing—check out *Networksolutions.com* and *Godaddy.com*.

Score A-List Public Relations on a Shoestring Budget, Part II

Public relations is free, however, it takes time and work. Are you ready?
As your PR expert, allow me to equip you with the necessary tools and continue the discussion on brand building for your multi-million dollar enterprise (speak into existence).

Now that you've begun to implement the steps from Part I: Score A-List Public Relations on a Shoestring Budget," here are additional tips used daily by successful business women and leaders:

Create content. Participate on the Web and promote your business unique quotient. Solidify your expert status in your respective field by creating a Blog (an online journal about your business) and Vlog (video blog which tells a story under three minutes). A great and economical resource is a Kodak Zi8 Pocket Video Camera in HD ($179.95).

Join a professional organization. Many national organizations in your respective profession have a local chapter—participate and become a member to enjoy the benefits of effective networking and pitching.

Promote your competition. If you are excellent at what you do then don't be afraid to promote the "other" company, to the media so you can become a resource of information and a tastemaker. For example: I promote other "experts" in my field since I operate from the principle that not everything is for me and what's for me is simply mine.

Hire a PR coach or expert. Turn to the experts to create a budget and plan that will masterfully help your media profile grow. An hourly rate or per project rate of $250 per hour (average cost), is well worth the investment in crafting a message, navigating the media maze and making introductions. Visit the National Black Public Relations Society for suggestions.

Advertise. The daily/weekly newspapers are battling economic woes and competition from the digital space and are in need of your business. Call an ad salesperson to determine a fiscally sound package to get your business out there and masterfully leverage a story in the deal.

Incorporate your tagline. Branding is about consistency and impressions. Use your e-mails to build brand awareness by promoting yourself as an expert each time. My tagline is "Karen Taylor Bass, The PR Expert."

Get feedback. Do they like the message? Is there any way to make it better? Try Survey Monkey to poll how your company is doing and to learn about the competition.

Lastly, just do it.

Re-Invention After The Storm

How do you re-invent, much less find the strength to get up and go on, after your son is fighting for life after being hurt by a drunk driver, and that driver happens to be his father?

Meet Joyce Adejumo. Her three-year old son Fred Leon "Mitchie" Mitchell was paralyzed below the waist as a result of his father driving drunk and crashing while returning him home after a weekend visitation. At that moment, everything stood still for Adejumo, who is divorced from Mitchie's father.

"Re-inventing is getting and picking up after everything has fallen apart. You declare to self that you will not fail, this won't kill me and a determination to succeed with faith and God's grace will ease the pain each day," says Adejumo.

How do you re-invent? By doing what you are called to do; be a catalyst for change and empower others in a similar situation. Re-invention can be a slow process, which requires a daily commitment to find your true authentic voice and ultimately act upon it.

Together Mitchie and Adejumo used this life-altering event as a way to educate the public, policymakers, and DWI offenders about the consequences of drunk driving and its debilitating impact on society. Their heart-wrenching story has made a tremendous impact on people, as well as a profound impact on public policy as it relates to DWI in Texas.

Adejumo started Mitchie's Fine Black Art and Gift Gallery in Austin, Texas, out of her house as a means of income when her son was injured, an outlet for Mitchie to use his hands and draw again, and to pursue her passion for art collectibles and books.

Mitchie died in 2007 as a result of complications from the 1989 crash.

"After months of struggling with the death of my only child, and the lawsuit with my ex-husband, I was at the end of my rope and broke down, released my grip on the pain, and surrendered to God," says Adejumo. "As God filled my emptiness and dried my tears, these prayers began flowing out of me on a daily basis—and I made a decision to capture them on paper by creating *My Daily Prayers: Spiritual Words of Wisdom Volume I*, knowing there were others going through life's storm and needed assurance that God is by their side regardless."

All proceeds from the book goes to The Mitchie Mitchell Foundation, which provides academic scholarships to high schools students who are survivors of accidents caused by drunk drivers and immediate family members of people injured or killed by drunk drivers. The foundation will donate five scholarships totaling $5,000 this year.

Although re-invention did not come lightly for Adejumo, her faithful stewardship and passion to help others has made Mitchie's Gallery a thriving business and meeting place for community activities. Adejumo and Mitchie's Gallery has received numerous community, state, and national service awards.

JOYCE ADEJUMO TIPS FOR RE-INVENTING AFTER THE STORM:
- **Be faithful.** Get silent and speak directly to God and allow him to provide you with strength and courage.
- **Be determined for a positive outcome.** It's not easy to have a positive attitude during the storm, however, if you believe - the message will be revealed for you to succeed.
- **Choose wisely.** The outcome to fail or succeed is within you, decide carefully what you want your legacy to be and simply understand that life is a gift and must be L-I-V-E-D one day at a time.

Are you in the process of re-inventing after a storm? What has helped you get through each day?

Social Media: The New Currency

Why women must be more aggressive about using networks to create business opportunities.

Social media is the new economy and game changer for getting your message out in cyberspace and beyond. If you have fresh ideas and the desire to try something new—get ready to grow your brand and be discovered.

You can amplify your message and grow your brand instantly by using popular networking tools such as Facebook, Twitter, LinkedIn, Ning, YouTube, and Animoto to name a few.

With social media you don't have to wait for a client or the media to discover your talent, service or goods. You can create platforms by engaging your friends, family and acquaintances by providing exceptional and creative content and messages via website, blog, Internet radio, and promotional videos.

African American women are using social media to influence brand loyalty and to increase popularity, however, many are not using social media to increase bottom-line as it relates to business.

According to Pam Perry, head of Ministry Marketing Solutions, "African American women think social media is a fad and for young kids, and don't realize people are making money with social media. Social media is a marketing tool and the quickest way to network and increase exposure for a brand. For social media to work you must target people that know and trust you."

As women we must understand that social media is the new currency, it's growing at an exponential rate, and if we don't master it now, we will be left behind. Men are using social media to create business opportunities and make money. Perry passionately asserts, "The difference, as it relates to gender, is that men are focused, deliver a clear and concise message, and are not afraid to make the 'ask' to close the deal. Women—more often than not—use social media as a popularity contest, send out random thoughts, and are afraid to promote their brand and make the 'ask.' "

Perry says, "People need to create the three F's to actively participate in social media:"

- **Followers:** People who like and trust you.
- **Friends:** People who will share your content, post comments, and rely on your message.
- **Fans:** People who will bookmark your blog or Website and will likely need giveaways and incentives to keep coming back.

The Internet is the greatest equalizer for women and other entrepreneurs to participate actively in birthing a new idea, engaging clients and increasing brand awareness, with a minimal investment cost. Let's change the perception of how black women do business by becoming savvier as it relates to social media.

SIX SOCIAL MEDIA STEPS TO BUILD AND PROMOTE YOUR BRAND

1. **Create a unique message about your brand/company** and share via social media platforms—Facebook, Twitter, Ning, LinkedIn, and YouTube.
2. **Build an online community** on the previously mentioned sites by always having something purposeful to say to engage your budding following. Use your existing relationships (family, friends, and colleagues) to build your fan base.
3. **Create a blog.** Blogging is your forum to provide an authentic commentary on a subject, combined with images and links, and allows you to interact with readers via their comments and your responses. If you are looking for maximum exposure and an indefinite shelf life for your material this is a smart starting point. (I recommend using Wordpress to start your blog).
4. **Become an Internet superstar with a viral video.** Create a slick informative commercial about your company that is no longer than 5 minutes long with a video camera and post it on YouTube, distribute it to your e-family, and solicit reviews. TV producers are in search of homemade commercials to discover "new" and "authentic" talent for TV programs and various media platforms.
5. **Host your own radio program.** I host a monthly program on *blogtalkradio.com*, which is free to set up, easy to produce, and a strategic way to promote your talent and expertise. Internet radio will improve your Google index when people search for your business/brand.
6. **Create a podcast on iTunes** to showcase your brand to potential clients. There are many free guides available online, but I recommend using the one created by Digital Trends.

Speed Networking: Brand and Promote in 2 Minutes

Are you ready to take your personal and business brand to the next level in record speed?

Get ready to try speed networking. Speed Networking is a creative way for entrepreneurs to meet substantial business contacts, secure referrals, and network in a friendly uplifting environment in a mere matter of hours.

Speed networking is often referenced as a spin-off to speed dating in a round-robin approach (attendees meet each other sequentially at a random pairing in a relaxed environment while displaying their best BRAND and expertise).

No need to worry if you are shy—no one cares—the object is to win and secure contacts!

Note: A common mistake entrepreneurs make when speed networking is not connecting with each participant. Don't look to score the BIG client—listen, engage and make the connection.

KAREN TAYLOR BASS' TIPS FOR EFFECTIVE SPEED NETWORKING:

Do's - Speed Networking:

- Prepare a smart and succinct 2 minutes brand pitch—engage your colleague and promote your expertise.
- Listen—often a lost art form, however, the best way to communicate and learn.
- Collect business cards and meet new colleagues.
- Engage, promote, and be the brand you want to be.
- Take notes—New Business contacts (write down key words to remember person for follow-up).
- Work the room during the reception to get out of your comfort zone.
- Follow-up with all potential contacts and referrals within 48 hours.

Don'ts:

- Poor Pitch—Make certain your pitch is interesting and include: name, company, title, tag line (what your business is known for), target audience, your niche and accolades.
- Lack of confidence—Believe in your brand each and every time.
- No follow-up—It is reported that 90% of business leads are not procured.

Yolanda Adams Gets Comfortable in Her Skin

Yolanda Adams is SEXY!
She is 50 years old, mother to Taylor and a 'brand' new mommy living her bliss marching to a new beat. Adams says, "I've always been comfortable with self and that's how I flow."

The art of balance escapes most of us; Yolanda Adams defines (her) balance as being able to work on her terms, enjoy family, and indulge in leisure without hassles.

We talked for 10 minutes and it was breezy, genuine and empowering. Adams is an accomplished multi-platinum Grammy® award winning singer, syndicated radio host, author, and now a clothing designer.

The foray into fashion was not taken lightly by Adams and the Yolanda Adams Collection was purposely planned with the best team of designers to create a product, which would offer the best knits and compete with designers St. John and Chanel for a reasonable price. Yolanda says, "It's been a lifetime of not being able to find clothes long enough to accommodate my height and I wanted to tailor to the exceptional woman, sizes 2-24.

Yolanda Adams Collection features a large selection of designer knits produced from the finest known yarn in America. YA Collection was founded to satisfy an unmet need in the fashion market—to generate silhouettes that are both flattering and wearable for the petite, plus size, and taller women while blending femininity with elegance.

"I've always loved clothing and when you are 16 years old and tall you get to sewing and creating that look, " says Adams.
Here are some questions TBNM asked Yolanda Adams:

TBNM: You have been blessed with motherhood, what are some of the challenges?
YA: I am self-employed and travel often. The most important thing is for my daughter to know that she is loved and I make all the important things – honor society, meetings, etc. I cherish Taylor and we have tons of fun, joke, and enjoy each other.

TBNM: One thing you can't live without?
YA: God and Daughter

TBNM: One thing that did not work in 2012 and you are giving it up for 2013?
YA: Everything in life works and when it doesn't I keep it moving. I celebrate everything that is possible—running, swimming, designing clothes and learn from my lessons.

YOLANDA ADAMS' TIPS FOR FOLKS SEEKING MOTIVATION TO RIDE OUT THE STORM
- Have a connection with God- he will keep you in spite of storm.
- Surround yourself with people who tell you that you will MAKE IT.
- Love family with all heart.
- Start doing what you absolutely love regardless of payment (storm will pass).
- Laugh and laugh so much.

Brand Mom: Tips to maximize 2.5 hours

No matter how you justify the expense, babysitting and day school is darn expensive for the preschoolers.

My little one (5 years), has been in a private day school since she was 17 months and this past September, we decided to take advantage of the free pre-Kindergarten in our district to save some MONEY. Just like you, the Bass family had to make some hard-line budgetary decisions and the verdict was send her to the FREE Pre-K in our district (which is quite good and ranks in the 90th percentile) to get some breathing room.

The only problem is FREE means FLEXIBILITY—the program is 2.5 hours of instructional learning and this 'brand' new momma has had to adjust to a new schedule of 'making it work' for all. Our older child is in junior high and since my work schedule is the most flexible, it was agreed I would do the drop-offs, pickups, after-school enrichment, homework, dinner, etc. which leaves me with 2.5 hours during the day to work and get it done for the brand new mommy/taylormade media brand.

Let me just say, it's challenging to be a successful entrepreneur, mom, wife, friend and maintain the damn sexy and meet deadlines. How do I do it? I exhale, order takeout twice a week, sip some wine a few mo' nights a week and work for 3 hours post bedtime.

HERE IS HOW I SPEND MY 2.5 HOURS DURING THE DAY:
- Get up early and meditate.
- Make a work plan and stick to it.
- Get moving. Take at least 30 minutes to workout.
- Make (2) biz calls, (1) new business and (1) follow-up.
- Compose and respond to emails for only 30 minutes.
- Tweet/Facebook responses for 10 minutes.
- Eat lunch.
- Go get your kids.

Date Yourself

Last weekend, I had the good fortune of presenting at the Blogging While Brown Conference in Los Angeles. It was a fantastic experience!

I presented with my BFF Pam Perry (Social Media guru) and during my module I mentioned the importance of dating yourself/brand in real time...all the time. Let's face it...you are your brand.

A brand is a consistent experience a consumer derive each time they come in contact with your product...think McDonald's french fries (they taste the same everywhere).

In any relationship, the energy will ultimately get stale/stagnant and the same thing will happen to your personal brand/you UNLESS you take the time to date and spend time with your brand.

Remember, when you were dating and everything around you appeared fresh? The birds chirped louder, the flowers appeared brighter, your eyes danced like a rock star, and your ideas overflowed like a monsoon?

Well, if that's not happening at this moment, it's time to go on a date with self. Here are my reasons why you should schedule a date night.

DATING SELF WILL ALLOW YOU TO:
- Renew and refresh your personal brand and self.
- Breathe fresh ideas into your business and relationships.
- Attract new customers/clients and friends.
- Allow you to see the big picture and NEVER give up.
- Empower you to laugh and have fun.
- Enjoy your amazing blessed life.

Are you ready to go out on a date?

Don't Give Away your M&Ms (Mind & Muscle)

I am an entrepreneur who is proud to finally say no more freebies to the vampires unless they are providing enrichment to my sphere and brand—be gone.

This was the year I decided to no longer giveaway my **M&Ms** (PR/Branding/Coaching expertise) for free because that would devalue my brand's worth and drain me.

Folks are crafty. Be mindful of one-way bartering, partnership, multi-level opportunities and so forth...you do your part but the other side comes up short.

Let me say it now—stop giving away your **M&Ms**.

Also, if people say I would like to work with you, B-U-T, let's see how it goes before anything is put in writing–proceed with extreme caution.

Don't make light of your intellectual property; come up with a price and billable hours menu to *ensure you don't get played*.

Make a rule that you will allocate (6) freebies a year to an organization, friend, charity, and will monetize the time, energy, transportation, it took to fulfill that obligation. I've learned this is the best way to understand and monetize your value so you don't feel like your blood has been sucked out.

If you are donating your services make certain its with a reputable organization and you get a letter stating your services and time for the IRS.

REMEMBER, YOUR M&M'S HAVE VALUE:
- If they weren't valuable folks would not ask you to donate your time, energy and expertise.
- Have them write you a formal letter with value for service as barter so you can have for tax purposes.
- If you don't value your **M&Ms** and make it known, no one else will.

New rule: You are playing to win; this is no longer a hobby.

What is "Kitty" Power, Do Moms Have It?

Do You Have "Kitty" Power?

Last Friday, I was having drinks with my girlfriends at the swank Mandarin Hotel at Columbus Circle in NYC—can you say ME Time!

While sipping my trademark Bellini cocktail (champagne and peach nectar puree), my friend, Leah, decided to drop some science.

Leah said, "Men have figured out how to walk into a room, command attention, make the pitch, and walk away with the deal…simply because most men believe they are the cats meow. She proceeded to say most women walk into the room, selling herself so hard, acting prim and proper, relying on how she is smarter than everyone else, but lacking the bravado to close the deal. Deepness!

Most women don't use or recognize their "Kitty" Power, it's their feminine gift, cat's meow, kitty kat…and it's their sex appeal, which brings out the confidence, strength, smarts, and bravada.

A woman with "Kitty" power knows what winning looks like and is not afraid to win without giving up any "Kitty."

So, I asked, who has this elusive "Kitty" power/juice?

Leah said, "Michelle Obama, Meryl Streep, Beyonce, Ellen DeGeneres, Jill Scott, Heidi Klum, Sarah Palin, Malinda Williams and Viola Davis and Jada Pinkett Smith," all have "kitty" power.

Leah continued to say, "A woman needs to walk into a room "kitty" first, show she is comfortable with her sexuality, pitch her business, and watch the men be thrown off their game expecting the unexpected. Having "Kitty" power is not giving anything up – it's using your feminine gift that comes from between the legs.

This got me to thinking … have most moms forgotten their "kitty kat power," after taking care of everyone all day, working a job, who the heck has time to channel "Kitty" power in Louboutin and pitch their business with sex appeal?

HERE ARE MY ACTIVITIES TO TAP INTO AND CHANNEL MY "KITTY" POWER:

- Sleep
- Pole Dancing
- Zumba
- Sexy Dressing
- Weight Lifting
- Doing grown stuff ... nuff said
- Letting stuff go and simply saying, "Forget It!"

How many of you are channeling your "Kitty" power and is it working for you?

JLO's Divorce 'Branding Tips

A marriage is a legal business contract—plain and simple.
It's easy to fantasize about romance, however, at the end of the day it's a business and like all partnerships sometimes they run their course.

For many, it was shocking when it was announced that Jennifer Lopez and Marc Anthony were calling it quits after seven years. Why?

Based upon what we've read in the media, Mr. Anthony wanted J.Lo to be another 'brand'...a less sexy version of herself.

Hmmm.

Remember, I always say that branding is about authenticity and when you allow others to define your WORTH and SELF there will be conflict and repercussions.

Jennifer Lopez is once again enjoying an infusion of energy and rejuvenation with her association of the 'Idol' brand...basically, she is pop culture relevant and feeling confident to make strategic decisions...like end a partnership which no longer works.

Jennifer Lopez is a courageous brand new mommy; she decided to renew and redefine her brand sans husband and live her authentic life as 'Jenny from the block.'

HERE IS WHAT WE CAN LEARN FROM BRAND JENNIFER LOPEZ:
- Know your self/brand authentically and LIVE it, even it cost you a relationship or business partnership.
- Self/inner peace is the most essential brand ingredient.
- Revaluate your business every 6 months and review what you need to eliminate or basically C-U-T.
- Be still and find YOUR voice.
- Strategic alliances can always resuscitate a stale brand.

ACT III : BLISS

It's that amazing feeling you get when all is good with you and no one can take the smile off your face.

Let me say that getting to bliss is not easy; I've experienced random acts of bliss in my life and work everyday to sustain a personal utopia.

Living for you: Maximize this weekend!

How do you plan on spending this weekend?
Shuttling back and forth between dance class, gymnastics, birthday parties, family responsibilities, cleaning, wifely duties etc?

Take a deep breath!

I have mastered the weekend hustle and still find a stolen moment to do what I want to do. How? Simply, by staying in the moment, being present and not anticipating the next activity.

I've recently learned when I stay in the moment —everyone has a great time—even me. Last weekend, the family went to the Hotel Hershey in Pennsylvania—it snowed; we became spontaneous and enjoyed the gift of snow.

Also, when you stay in the moment it really becomes about you and no one else; you are allowing self to be still, engaged and not plan the next scene in your mind.

TIPS TO MAXIMIZE YOUR WEEKEND AND (STILL) HAVE A GREAT TIME:
- **Do one thing!** Be clear what your goal is for the weekend and share with "team." Is the goal to clean, chill, arts/crafts etc?
- **Work out!** I went to the Hotel Hershey last weekend and worked out one day with my 11 year old and the next morning took a sunrise yoga class all for me.
- **Indulge.** Eat your fave food with no apologies in moderation.
- **Smooch.** You and your sweetie both need love.
- **Enjoy!** Life is too short not to have a great weekend; it's all up to you.

Commit to having fun, staying in the moment and mastering one thing at a time.

Divinely Imperfectly Imbalance is the New Black!

Being imperfect is the new black; you don't have to have it all together.
Think about your parents and how they did not have it together when you were growing up; however, all the valuable lessons you learned in the process?

Trial and error still rocks!

I read a blog by a popular celebrity-mom talking about how she is able to manage all three of her kids, workout, have dinner prepared at 6pm, schedule date night twice a week and still hang-out with girlfriends for coffee or wine?

Wow, that's darn impressive!! Most weeks, I order takeout 2x, check homework, kiss my husband and pass out on the couch in my sweats.

Then I did some research and learned that this 'certain' celebrity has a "team," not just a "nanny" to keep her and family together.

It's all about being authentic and telling people what's going on truthfully and not feeling compelled to create perfection—it does not exist regardless of your income.

So what if you have not lost all the weight gained during pregnancy and it took Mariah Carey 3 months to lose 30 pounds? She is a paid Jenny Craig spokesperson! If you were getting paid to lose weight you would put down that piece of chicken, I know I would.

It's time to stop the madness and not use celebrity as the barometer in our lives to measure success. Remember, they are only telling you the "PR" friendly parts of the 'brand'.

I've learned it's okay to be imperfectly imbalanced and not play into what I am supposed to say.

When we couldn't afford to send our daughter to an elite day school this school year (she has always gone since 17 months) because it was so darn expensive, she went to the FREE Pre-K in the district. Immediately my circle of moms asked why she was registered to attend and I authentically said, **"Not in the budget this year."** At that moment, several moms in the circle confessed that they too were struggling.

Brand New Mommy Bliss Tip: Timing is Everything…Can't Rush Process

BNM, how are you today?

This morning I went into the backyard and really observed the process of a flower opening. It's quite miraculous.

If you pay close attention–the stalks grow first, then the leaves and each day a hint of what will eventually become a flower. Wow! Life is so beautiful when you slow down and realize that all the sowing of your personal seeds, thoughts, ideas, and watering them with love and encouragement, will eventually open up to something ordained and authentic.

I've learned that just because I want my sunflower to bloom it won't open up until it's ready. Deepness! Just like I've signed contracts about projects but nothing goes according to plan until the universe says, "Let's make it happen."

Timing is everything, simply can't rush the process to get to the finish line.

The waiting prepares us for the #gift.

What are you trying to rush, BNM?

Celebrate Valentine's Day with Mommy Self-Love!

As we get ready for Valentine's Day, nothing beats love than SELF-LOVE!
This is the tine for all moms to finally say enough is enough and put self-first. Celebrating Valentine's Day with a twist of mommy love me day!

Moms are always taking care of the world and this year let's plan to put self first boldly and embrace a brand new you and become– renewed and redefined to work on personal BRAND!

Brand New Look. It's time for a change! If your like me and have had the same look and style for over 20 years, let's commit to a new hairstyle and unleash the inner fabulosity.

Brand New Body. Get moving and commit to take a Yoga, Zumba or Salsa class. This year let's do new things and first up - a better mind, body and soul.

Take the 'ultimate' class. This is the best time to channel your inner passion and be the chef, writer, teacher, actress and 'brand.' Sign up for a class at a neighborhood college/university.

Celebrate Mommy Love. Select a day each month to celebrate motherhood by being still, meditating and honor self by carving out one hour each month to pamper you—the 'brand' new mommy.

Spa. Take yourself to spa or a manicure/pedicure and allow someone to pamper all your greatness.

Gratitude: Give Some and Get Some

Gratitude.
Give thanks and get on your knees and thank your higher power for today.
Yes, it's not perfect, you've been asking and pleading for a miracle and nothing yet. I know.
In full disclosure, I have experienced so many emotions since I became a mom: anxiety, stress, depression, hope, love, renewal, reinvention and discovery of self (again).
Give praise and thanks for all that is about to happen—it will be great, not good.
Belief is crucial in the art of gratitude.
'Brand' New Mommy, the darkness will give to light, therefore, at this moment give thanks for anticipation. You have crafted an amazing campaign, networked with movers and shakers and taken all the steps for a successful brand/campaign.
I prayed for a MIRACLE (ad nauseam) and had to give it up to gratitude for all that would eventually come. God remembers all our requests.
The late Nora Ephron said, "Even when I see blemishes on my skin, I give thanks for the gift of seeing them." Wow.
I want you to walk with me in the spirit of renewal. Trust self that all will be divine and turn it over to a higher power today. Trust, faith, praise and give thanks.
Give gratitude for all you have and will accomplish, lessons learned, health, mind, spirit and laughter.
Life is a gift. Send up your praise for each day for the miracle of life.
Give gratitude!

When was the last time you simply gave gratitude?

Moms: Need Personal Time Too

Ommmm!
It's a simple word to chant and if done correctly can bring serenity to one's space, feeling and life.

The Queens/LI Mochas came in with the hustle and bustle of the outside world a few Saturdays ago; stress, children, career, juggling, life balance and working diligently to stay in the moment.

Although, the Mochas tried to just walk into the space with shoes on all the feeling of the 'outside' world, it was the tranquility of Kashmir Hands, which set the tone for-let go…let flow.

What an (almost) impossible fete for Mochas—until they walked into Kashmir Hands to enjoy an evening of yoga.

"Take your shoes off and let yourself enjoy the space," said Dina Giugliano.

It was at that moment, 16 ladies transformed and gave themselves to the moment—got still and allowed body to become aligned, usher in peace, purge toxins and just be.

Dina, the yoga guru said, "push, push and allow your body to take you there and most of all stay in the moment. This is your practice, not your neighbor."

After 75 minutes of deep breathing it was pure bliss, less stress and Zen for all Mochas.

Mocha Sanya said, "I needed this gift; and, Mocha Stephanie said, "This session was sooo relaxing, I almost need a nap."

Yes Mochas, Namaste'!

Breathing is a gift

Are you breathing?
It sounds simple but many of us are not breathing—simply moving.
Is that you?
Breathing takes time; each conscious inhalation and exhalation has to be deliberate and when we take the time to do it, life is enjoyed, blissful, and purposeful and greatness is actualized.

Everyone expects much from The Brand New Mommy and Daddy; however, we must tell people that we need a moment to **breathe**.

Yesterday, I went and got a massage from Surreal Serenity in Queens, New York and was completely turned out. For two plus hours I was breathing in perfect health; confidence, love, life, beauty, and pampering my core—that one session gave me a night of pure bliss and great sleep.

My gift to self from now on is to simply breathe and get a massage once a month for preservation.

Let's do it together—breathe in, hold it, and release all those toxins. ***Do this again at least 3 times to get back to center.***

Sending Brand New Mommy Love!

Countdown to 8:30

Are you a happy mother?

I was watching NBC Today Show with Kathie Lee and Hoda and the guest was a doctor talking about the 10 healthy habits of healthy moms and how we should reclaim our joys as women and not feel guilty.

Thank you—finally the truth about how guilty we feel and why we must come first (although it's a daily practice for me).

Let me be honest with you and say that I countdown to 8:30pm each night to begin Act II. For me, 8:30pm is that magic bedtime number when my kids are getting ready for bed or already in a sweet slumber and mommy can have a PRIVATE P-A-R-T-Y!

Yes, I love my children, however, like you—work, meetings, reviewing homework, taking Sofia/Sebastian to after-school activities, and enjoying a uniquely different bedtime routine for my kids (ages 3.5 and 11)—is a lot on most days.

Mommy needs her medicine most nights after 8:30pm when the kids are sleeping—my favorite glass of Sebeka red wine.

HERE IS WHAT HAPPENS AFTER 8:30PM FOR THIS MOMMY:

- I take a deep breath and thank God for my family.
- Face time with my hubby.
- A relaxation bath with Vera Moore Spa set (sugar scrub is the joint).
- Write in my journal.
- TV (General Hospital on SoapNet OR The Game/Law & Order/The Good Wife).
- Review my vision board and meditate.
- Prayers and play a CD to help me savor the moments of the day.

What happens in your household after 8:30pm?

Celebrate your bliss!

Happy March—it's time to celebrate you for Women's History Month.
Brand New Mommy, Sister, She-roe, Entrepreneur, Single Lady,—I love you for your passion, perseverance, pride, zeal and your style to get this done.

I challenge you to celebrate for the next 31 days (March) your gift to everyone you touch, encounter, mentor, care for, and worry about.

It's time to have fun!

HERE ARE A FEW SUGGESTIONS TO CELEBRATE (YOUR) WOMEN'S HISTORY MONTH:
- Pray each morning at the same time for consistency. Give it all to the Lord.
- Do little treats 30 out of 31 days—sleep in, park your car and walk, and freakin' say No (just because).
- Prepare to blast-off your brand with a real plan.
- Celebrate a Black-owned business each day with a purchase/support/ encouragement mentality.
- Meet your girlfriends for cocktails and laugh like you are 21 (again).
- Be naughty and nice!
- Wear a color (red, orange, green, yellow, and purple) and show off your beautiful hue.
- Make a video celebrating the people in your life with *Animoto.com*.
- Add this phrase to your vision board—"Success Is An Inside Job"
- Pare down your debt and skip Starbucks for 5 days this month.

I Am Thankful

I can't believe that the holiday season is upon us.
What the heck happened to the year?
Don't you remember making a resolution several months ago? I do...this year was filled with growth, evolution, and challenges. Through it all, I stayed in the climb and saw many dreams crystallized.

With the season for giving in full swing don't let the pressure take over, you know... pandemonium, gift giving, parties, shopping, going into debt, depression, anxiety, unemployment, and dreams deferred.

Enjoy the free stuff in life...breathing, loving, and smiling.
I am thankful for my health this season.

- *Health.* Simply being with no pain and medication.
- *Movement.* Going for a walk, breathing, creating ideas, driving my car, moving my arms, no back pain, having my legs dance, and daydreaming at my neighborhood park.
- *My mind.* Yes, there are times when I am on overload and can't remember my pin number; however, at the core of it all I am still sharp and appreciative of the gift of life.

This season I am not looking for a turquoise blue jewelry box or anything fantabulous–just the birth of another year and continued peace, spirit, health, love, and joy.

I know it sounds crazy but with so many (younger) people around me dealing with health challenges all I want is to BE and enjoy each moment.

Happy Thanksgiving!

Why we Love Our Girlfriends

A true girlfriend is a rare gem and if you are blessed–you will have a few really really good ones. Let's face it, not all girlfriends are good... like not all Black folks are Black.

12 years ago, I met Aisha, Syreeta and Jill through work and we slowly became friends.

When I first met them it was my intention not to become too close since we were all working together (why do we do that?) and did not want to co-mingle work and friendship.

I was successful for two years keeping them in a "box" and then we went on a retreat together in the deep woods of West Virginia and I allowed my wall to collapse.

It was then I accepted it was okay to be friends with a future superstar, a budding entrepreneur, and an Ivy League graduate. Our friendship has weathered many storms, joys, truths, sorrows, and the ultimate blessing of motherhood. Through it all, we have been there for each other and always promised never to judge.

Black women are guarded and many are taught not to trust; that weekend I put all my business on front street and cried with my girlfriends as they did the same. We created our vision board that weekend and in a mere matter of years each dream became fulfilled. Last week, we laughed, and said it was time to go on another retreat and create a new vision board and this time to dream gargantuan and raise the bar. This is why I love my girlfriends.

WE LOVE OUR GIRLFRIENDS BECAUSE:
- They know us better than your mates
- We can have girlie moments
- They don't pass judgment
- A true BFF will want the best for you
- Titles and roles are not important
- Love is unconditional

Dear 'Brand' New Mommy,

I love you!

I am writing this letter to you as a reminder that you are the BOMB DOT COM and uniquely fabulous.

Starting today, you will kick the S#@T to the curb which no longer works and begin to live and love your bliss.

Take the next 5 minutes to write a love letter to self and plan to spend 10 minutes a day simply enjoying all that you are.

_____
_____
_____
_____
_____
_____
_____
_____
_____
_____
_____
_____
_____
_____

With Love,

About The Author

Karen Taylor Bass, The Brand New Mommy & PR Expert

Considered one of the premier authorities in the public relations industry, Karen Taylor Bass, has created strategic "out of the box," public relations, branding, and marketing campaigns for celebrities, athletes, entrepreneurs, and corporations for over 15 years.

Now she spends her time as the PR Expert/TaylorMade Media and CEO of *TheBrandNewMommy.com*, a digital destination for savvy women renewing and redefining their personal brand post childbirth.

Taylor Bass is an author, public relations coach, brand consultant, and a popular host for *Brand: Mom* on *Chic Rebellion. TV.*

She has appeared on numerous media outlets: The Nate Berkus Show, NBC Today New York, NBC-10! (Philly), WDAS-FM, BET News, *CNN.com*, Fox-TV Chicago, CBS-NY, Café Mocha Radio (nationally syndicated), *Newsday, Black Enterprise, The Network Journal, Essence, Ebony, The Grio.com, Philadelphia Daily News, Philadelphia Tribune, New York Daily News,* and countless others.

Taylor Bass' ability to visualize the big picture and develop short and long term initiatives while developing and cultivating niche markets makes her the undisputed Brand New Mommy and PR Expert.

You can learn more about Taylor Bass by visiting *www.taylormademediapr.com*, *www.karentaylorbass.com*, and *www.thebrandnewmommy.com*.

> **'Brand' New Mommy**
> *Essential Resources*

BABIES

The March of Dimes
www.marchofdimes.com

Breastfeeding
www.laleche.org/

Mocha Moms
www.mochamoms.org

POST PARTUM

www.postpartum.net

BRANDING

The Brand New Mommy
www.thebrandnewmommy.com

BLISS

Yoga
www.yoga.com

Spa
www.spafinder.com

Order Information

TaylorMade Books are available at quantity discounts with bulk purchases for educational, business and sales promotional use. For information, please contact:

TaylorMade Books
c/o The Brand New Mommy: From Babies To Branding To Bliss
info@thebrandnewmommy.com
www.thebrandnewmommy.com

www.ingramcontent.com/pod-product-compliance
Lightning Source LLC
Chambersburg PA
CBHW021019090426
42738CB00007B/828